Teaming and Collaboration

DEC Recommended Practices Monograph Series

DEC Recommended Practices:
Enhancing Services for Young Children With Disabilities and Their Families

Environment:
Promoting Meaningful Access, Participation, and Inclusion

Family:
Knowing Families, Tailoring Practices, Building Capacity

Instruction:
Effective Strategies to Support Engagement, Learning, and Outcomes

Interaction:
Enhancing Children's Access to Responsive Interactions

Teaming and Collaboration:
Building and Sustaining Partnerships

Teaming and Collaboration

Building and Sustaining Partnerships

DEC Recommended Practices Monograph Series

Division for Early Childhood
of the Council for Exceptional Children

Washington, DC

Disclaimer

Published and Distributed by:

Division for
Early
Childhood
of the Council for Exceptional Children

E-mail: dec@dec-sped.org
Website: http://www.dec-sped.org/

The Division for Early Childhood (DEC), a division of the Council for Exceptional Children, is an international membership organization for individuals who work with or on behalf of young children with disabilities and other special needs. Founded in 1973, DEC's mission is to promote policies and advance evidence-based practices that support families and enhance the optimal development of young children who have or are at risk for developmental delays and disabilities. Information about membership and other resources available can be found at www.dec-sped.org

Editors: Pamela J. Winton, *University of North Carolina at Chapel Hill*, Chelsea Guillen, *University of Illinois at Urbana-Champaign*, and Alana G. Schnitz, *Juniper Gardens Children's Project*
Copy editing and cover and interior design: Kevin Dolan
Indexer: Jean Jesensky, *Endswell Indexing*
Typeset in Warnock Pro, Myriad Pro, and Calibri
All photos provided by iStock except those provided by the Frank Porter Graham Child Development Institute on pages 69, 72, 78, 81, and 112 and those submitted by authors of their article on pages 111 and 115.

Suggested Citation

Winton, P. J., Guillen, C., & Schnitz, A. G. (Eds.). (2019). *Teaming and collaboration: Building and sustaining partnerships* (DEC Recommended Practices Monograph Series No. 6). Washington, DC: Division for Early Childhood.

TABLE OF CONTENTS

of the Council for Exceptional Children

Download the DEC Recommended Practices
www.dec-sped.org/
dec-recommended-practices

Teaming and Collaboration
The Centerpiece of Early Intervention/ Early Childhood Special Education

PAMELA J. WINTON
University of North Carolina at Chapel Hill

CHELSEA GUILLEN
University of Illinois at Urbana-Champaign

ALANA G. SCHNITZ
Juniper Gardens Children's Project

WORKING COLLABORATIVELY WITH FAMILIES AND OTHER PRO-fessionals is part of the DNA of most professionals who identify as early interventionists and early childhood special educators. The reasons why are multiple and relate to the origins of the profession as well as the historic legislative support for interdisciplinary, family-centered, inclusionary approaches to service delivery to young children with disabilities and their families.

In its beginnings, the field of early intervention (EI)/early childhood special education (ECSE) was composed of professionals from a range of disciplines (e.g., psychology, education, special education, child and human development, mental health, social work; see McLean, Sandall, & Smith [2016] for more information on the history of the field). These early leaders brought with them to the relatively new field of EI/ECSE different sources of knowledge, philosophical traditions, standards for practice, and policy guidelines. By virtue of their commitment to join forces across disciplinary boundaries to work with and respond to the variety of needs of young children with disabilities and their families, the early leaders were plunged into an environment where the practices of teaming and collaborating with others were a necessary skill set. These historical origins continue to influence the field and have led to teaming and collaboration being an undergirding value of the EI/ECSE field.

Teaming and collaboration practices also have had strong legislative support over time. The early leaders' recognition that the needs of young children with disabilities and their families, especially infants and toddlers, are best addressed as early as possible and by an interdisciplinary approach has shaped policies. The Education of the Handicapped Act Amendments of 1986 (PL 99-457) extended the requirement for states to provide services for children with disabilities down to preschoolers and established incentives for states to provide services for

DEC Recommended Practices Commissioners

Mary McLean, chair
Rashida Banerjee
Tricia Catalino
Chelsea Guillen
Kathy Hebbeler
Anne Larson
Tara McLaughlin
Lori Erbrederis Meyer
Brian Reichow
Beth Rous
Susan Sandall
Sheila Self
Pat Snyder
Judy Swett
Pam Winton

Past Commissioners

Barbara J. Smith,
    past chair
Judy Carta
Mary Louise Hemmeter

children birth through age 2. Regulations under the Individuals With Disabilities Education Act (2004) stipulated that services and supports be provided in the least restrictive environment for preschoolers and in natural environments for infants and toddlers. This further reinforced the importance of collaboration between those in the child's natural environment (e.g., families, early care and education teachers) and specialists in allied health, special education, and other disciplines.

Interdisciplinary competencies for early intervention were identified in the late 1980s (Bailey, Buysse, & Palsha, 1990). They became the foundation for standards that still guide the EI/ECSE field today (Bruder, 2016). Additionally, in the early 1990s, teacher education programs were challenged to make structural changes to reflect the continued emphasis on teaming and collaboration, especially within the context of inclusive services (Miller & Stayton, 1998). Competitive, discretionary grants for personnel preparation programs from the U.S. Department of Education's Office of Special Education Programs (OSEP) began to include funding priorities that encouraged interdisciplinary approaches. As a result, some institutes of higher education merged ECE and EI/ECSE coursework and programs that had previously been administratively housed in separate departments. This approach has endured over time with a number of early childhood teacher education programs engaging faculty from different disciplinary backgrounds to prepare students to work as part of teams serving children in natural and inclusive settings (Bruder, 2016; Grisham-Brown & Hemmeter, 2017; Kilgo, Vogtle, Aldridge, & Ronilo this monograph). A corollary development was that content related to teaming and collaboration practices became recognized as important to include in preservice and in-service curricula (Guillen & Winton, 2015; Kilgo & Bruder, 1997; Sexton, Snyder, Lobman, Kimbrough, & Matthews, 1997).

The fact that teaming and collaboration is one of eight key topic areas in the current DEC Recommended Practices (Division for Early Childhood, 2014) is a reflection of the field's origins and long-standing values, the legislative priority for interdisciplinary and family-centered approaches to service delivery, and funding opportunities for programs engaged in interdisciplinary approaches to personnel preparation and professional development.

Overview of Teaming and Collaboration Practices and Research Related to Them

Although teaming and collaboration are at the forefront of intervention and practice with young children and their families, there is relatively little rigorous research related to the practices in ECSE. As such, it is important to look to the larger body of other disciplines such as early childhood mental health, adult learning theory and psychological sciences.

Because children with disabilities and their families often have multiple professionals working in partnership with them, it is important that they come together to make data-based decisions to guide interventions for children as recommended by TC1. The literature on TC1 provides information on strategies that support team effectiveness (Cohen & Bailey, 1997; West, Brodbeck,

& Richter, 2004) and the importance of using data to guide decision making in early childhood (Akers et al., 2016; Giangreco, 1995). TC2 encourages team members to share their expertise with one another—exchanging information; planning jointly; engaging in observation, modeling, and reflecting; and providing performance feedback. For example, Brookman-Frazee, Stahmer, Lewis, Feder, and Reed (2012) describe a researcher-practitioner partnership and teaming strategies used with families to improve outcomes for infants and toddlers diagnosed with autism spectrum disorder. TC2 stresses the importance of all members of the team sharing information and giving feedback to each other to increase positive outcomes for children.

TC3 focuses on the group processes that enhance team functioning and the relationships among team members. There is an expansive literature on this topic, and recommendations include having team members who are knowledgeable in their area of focus; creating shared goals; using data to guide intervention planning; celebrating accomplishments; and encouraging open, honest, and clear communication (Bell, 2007; Flowers, Mertens, & Mulhall, 1999; Hunt, Soto, Maier, Liboiron, & Bae, 2004). TC4 encourages teams to identify and use community-based supports and organizations to meet family-identified needs. It is important to consider each family's unique needs and values when considering interventions. Horner, Dunlap, and Koegel (1988) and contributors to their edited book detail the supports families need to continue to use interventions over time and across contexts such as ongoing support, community resources, and explicit instruction in multiple contexts. The final Teaming and Collaboration recommended practice, TC5, encourages teams to work together to support families and children by choosing a primary liaison to support families. When choosing the primary liaison, it is important to understand and consider the family and child as well as environmental and practitioner factors that may affect progress and successful implementation of interventions with families and children (Shonkoff, Hauser-Cram, Krauss, & Upshur, 1992; Sloper, Greco, Beecham, & Webb, 2006). Together the literature provides insight on factors and effective strategies that promote teaming and collaboration around supports for young children.

Current Trends That Support Teaming and Collaboration

Despite the long-standing set of values, legislative focus, and research on teaming and collaboration, many early childhood professionals still struggle to partner with families and other professionals (Rush, Shelden, & Hanft, 2003). Some promising new support for teaming and collaboration comes from early childhood professional organizations and federal agencies. One example is the development of joint position statements. The Division for Early Childhood (DEC) and the National Association for the Education of Young Children (NAEYC), two national professional organizations focused on young children and their families, collaborated in 2009 on a position paper to identify "the types of practices and supports necessary to achieve high quality inclusion." Recommendations for how to implement inclusion to improve early childhood services are included in the position statement, and all recommendations include some level of teaming and collaboration. Another example of professional organization support for improving teaming and collaboration is the current Power to the Profession initiative (https://www.naeyc.org/our-work/initiatives/profession). This initiative brings together a number of national organizations to define and provide support for the early childhood profession. This effort aims to bring consistency to the field and unify standards and competencies for those who work with young children and their families, goals that can facilitate enhanced teaming and collaboration across systems.

Federal agencies also continue to support teaming by modeling collaboration in the development of joint policy statements that outline expectations for teaming and collaboration. Two examples are the U.S. Departments of Health and Human Services and Education joint policy statements on inclusion (2015) and home visiting (2017). Both of these statements set a vision and provide recommendations for how states can partner, coordinate, and collaborate on behalf of young children with disabilities. Federal initiatives such as the Child Care Development Block Grant and the Early Head Start-Child Care Partnership encourage collaboration across early childhood systems and settings by requiring grantees to elaborate on how they will implement services for children in multiple programs. These efforts provide additional impetus for teaming and collaboration as they include not only expectations but resources to support the federal vision.

Overview of Articles

The articles in this monograph illustrate the variety of settings and contexts in which teaming and collaboration practices play a critical role. The first six articles focus on local community-based programs as the context for collaboration and teaming. In the first article, Lieberman-Betz, Wiegand, Brown, and Vail provide important background information on the topic, including defining models of teaming and a rationale for why collaboration is important. Through an illustrative vignette of an early intervention team working with a child with cerebral palsy and her family, they focus on strategies for communication, especially when working with families who are diverse. The context for the next article, by Luke, is on a child diagnosed with autism spectrum disorder who is transitioning from an early intervention program to an inclusive preschool classroom. This article's unique contribution is the description of the use of technology to promote communication among the professionals and family members who support the child's successful adjustment and progress in her new environment. In their article, Towson and Green describe a collaboration approach called appreciative inquiry (AI). They illustrate how the AI approach helps a speech language pathologist support a paraprofessional's use of dialogic reading in a prekindergarten classroom. Through the case illustration, this article provides important details about how team members enhance their knowledge about both the AI approach and the strategies for using dialogic reading.

Shannon, Bishop, Snyder, and Jaramillo describe how the successful implementation of components of practice-based coaching by a Head Start disabilities coordinator not only supported Head Start teachers' implementation of embedded interventions with a child with an IEP but also supported the development of collaborative partnerships among the team of professionals. Tools and strategies associated with practice-based coaching are shared with specific details about how their use in the classroom helped promote teaming and collaboration practices among the professionals involved. The article by Weglarz-Ward describes teaming and collaboration practices that promote the partnership between an early interventionist and an early childhood teacher. The author shares tips for planning early intervention services in child care settings and includes a table outlining roles and responsibilities across early childhood agencies and parents related to the early intervention process, including screening, referrals, evaluation, and service delivery.

The final article in this section of the monograph by Pedonti, Lim, Winton, Becton, and Wiggins addresses the challenges of communitywide collaboration among different early childhood agencies whose missions support the inclusion of young children with disabilities in natural and inclusive environments. The article provides details about how the budding relationship between two individuals working in different community agencies (Head Start and the local education agency) provided a catalyst for the development of teaming and collaboration practices at both the program and community levels. Specific tools and strategies developed as a result of the collaboration (e.g., therapy logs used to communicate with parents, teachers, and specialists) are described.

The next section of the monograph, consisting of four articles, focuses on statewide technical assistance and professional development models that support the growth of teaming and collaboration practices. Romano et al. describe an ambitious statewide interagency project designed to promote the implementation of the DEC Recommended Practices as one strategy for ensuring high-quality family-centered early intervention services across the state of Iowa. With a particular focus on the Teaming and Collaboration recommended practices, the authors provide details about the challenges and successes experienced by the project's three education districts. They include lessons learned, one being that "a unified vision does not necessarily require a single path." Rendon and Schnurr, also working in the state of Iowa, describe a statewide project designed to promote teaming and collaboration among Early Head Start and early intervention leaders and providers. Working with 11 different community-based teams over a 14-month period, they learned about the processes necessary for collaborative partnerships to flourish and implemented strategies to support collaboration. They include a self-assessment tool for teams to use to gauge their progress and identify action steps for improving collaboration across the essential components of the early intervention process.

Ropars and Kremer, working in the context of a statewide training and technical assistance program in Illinois that supports high-quality inclusive services, describe the development and implementation of a team-based professional development series. One of the unique contributions of this article is how the authors used the Inclusive Classroom Profile (Soukakou, 2012) as a self-assessment tool to help teams identify areas of strength and needed improvements in their inclusive preschool programs. They provide details about the design and strategies used in the implementation of a professional development experience in a community-based pilot site. In the concluding article of this section of the monograph, Kilgo, Vogtle, Aldridge, and Ronilo address the important role pre-service programs play in preparing professionals to learn about and implement teaming and collaboration practices. They describe the interprofessional graduate-level program they have developed and sustained for almost 20 years at a state university. They include concrete teaching strategies that provide students the opportunity to apply what they have learned and get feedback from faculty and peers. The final article in the monograph provides rich descriptions of a collection of resources on teaming and collaboration, some new and some classics that are as relevant today as they were when first developed several decades ago.

The articles in this issue identify a number of challenges to successful teaming and collaboration and provide examples of how some of these challenges can be overcome. Examples of challenges include finding time for, and scheduling, meetings where teams can come together to share knowledge and expertise; reimbursing team members for time spent collaborating with other adults; misconceptions about other programs' requirements and responsibilities; differences in program/system terminology; limited valuing of the information other team members have; lack of support or opportunities for cross-agency or interdisciplinary professional development; and maintaining privacy and confidentiality. Examples in the articles of how these challenges can be addressed include use of secure technology, development and implementation of interagency agreements and/or memorandums of understanding, transdisciplinary preservice preparation, prioritization of communication and time for teaming and reflection, joint service planning and visits, information sharing about program purpose and requirements, and innovative professional development initiatives. Many of the individual articles include resources that teams can use to support their communication and group facilitation efforts.

In summary, it is important to note that in every article the power of individual relationships is highlighted as a key to collaboration and teaming. While challenges persist, the articles illustrate how focused efforts with others who believe in the benefits of information exchange between families and professionals, collective expertise, and using data to guide decisions can result in improved teaming and collaboration across individuals, programs, and systems.

References

Akers, L., Del Grosso, P., Snell, E., Atkins-Burnett, S., Wasik, B. A., Carta, J., . . . Monahan, S. (2016). Tailored teaching: Emerging themes from the literature on teachers' use of ongoing child assessment to individualize instruction. *NHSA Dialog, 18*, 133–150.

Bailey, D. B., Jr., Buysse, V., & Palsha, S. A. (1990). Self-ratings of professional knowledge and skills in early intervention. *Journal of Special Education, 23*, 423–435, doi:10.1177/002246699002300406

Bell, S. T. (2007). Deep-level composition variables as predictors of team performance: A meta-analysis. *Journal of Applied Psychology, 92*, 595–615. doi:10.1037/0021-9010.92.3.595

Brookman-Frazee, L., Stahmer, A. C., Lewis, K., Feder, J. D., & Reed, S. (2012). Building a research-community collaborative to improve community care for infants and toddlers at-risk for autism spectrum disorders. *Journal of Community Psychology, 40,* 715–734. doi:10.1002/jcop.21501

Bruder, M. B. (2016). Personnel development practices in early childhood intervention. In B. Reichow, B. A. Boyd, E. E. Barton, & S. L. Odom (Eds.), *Handbook of early childhood special education* (pp. 289–333). Cham, Switzerland: Springer.

Cohen, S. G., & Bailey, D. E. (1997). What makes teams work: Group effectiveness research from the shop floor to the executive suite. *Journal of Management, 23,* 239–290. doi:10.1177/014920639702300303

DEC/NAEYC. (2009). *Early childhood inclusion: A joint position statement of the Division for Early Childhood (DEC) and the National Association for the Education of Young Children (NAEYC).* Chapel Hill: The University of North Carolina.

Division for Early Childhood. (2014). *DEC recommended practices in early intervention/early childhood special education 2014.* Retrieved from http://www.dec-sped.org/dec-recommended-practices

Flowers, N., Mertens, S. B., & Mulhall, P. F. (1999). The impact of teaming: Five research-based outcomes. *Middle School Journal, 31*(2), 57–60. doi:10.1080/00940771.1999.11494619

Giangreco, M. (1995). Related services decision-making: A foundational component of effective education for students with disabilities. *Physical and Occupational Therapy in Pediatrics, 15*(2), 47–68. doi:10.1080/J006v15n02_04

Grisham-Brown, J., & Hemmeter, M. L. (Eds.). (2017). *Blended practices for teaching young children in inclusive settings* (2nd ed.). Baltimore, MD: Paul H. Brookes.

Guillen, C., & Winton, P. (2015). Teaming and collaboration: Thinking about how as well as what. In Division for Early Childhood, *DEC recommended practices: Enhancing services for young children with disabilities and their families* (DEC Recommended Practices Monograph Series No. 1; pp. 99–108). Los Angeles, CA: Division for Early Childhood.

Horner, R. H., Dunlap, G., & Koegel, R. L. (Eds.). (1988). *Generalization and maintenance: Life-style changes in applied settings.* Baltimore, MD: Paul H. Brookes.

Hunt, P., Soto, G., Maier, J., Liboiron, N., & Bae, S. (2004). Collaborative teaming to support preschoolers with severe disabilities who are placed in general education early childhood programs. *Topics in Early Childhood Special Education, 24,* 123–142. doi:10.1177/02711214040240030101

Individuals With Disabilities Education Act, 20 U.S.C. § 1400 (2004).

Kilgo, J. L., & Bruder, M. B. (1997). Creating new visions in institutions of higher education: Interdisciplinary approaches to personnel preparation in early intervention. In P. J. Winton, J. A. McCollum, & C. Catlett (Eds.), *Reforming personnel preparation in early intervention: Issues, models, and practical strategies* (pp. 81–102). Baltimore, MD: Paul H. Brookes.

McLean, M., Sandall, S. R, & Smith, B. J. (2016). A history of early childhood special education. In B. Reichow, B. A. Boyd, E. E. Barton, & S. Odom (Eds.), *Handbook of early childhood special education* (pp. 3–19). Cham, Switzerland: Springer.

Miller, P. S., & Stayton, V. D. (1998). Blended interdisciplinary teacher preparation in early education and intervention: A national study. *Topics in Early Childhood Special Education, 18,* 49–58. doi:10.1177/027112149801800108

Rush, D. D., Shelden, M. L., & Hanft, B. E. (2003). Coaching families and colleagues: A process for collaboration in natural settings. *Infants and Young Children, 16,* 33–47.

Sexton, J. D., Snyder, P., Lobman, M., Kimbrough, P., & Matthews, K. (1997). A team-based model to improve early intervention programs: Linking preservice and inservice. In P. J. Winton, J. McCollum, & C. Catlett (Eds.), *Reforming personnel preparation in early intervention: Issues, models, and practical strategies* (pp. 495–526). Baltimore, MD: Paul H. Brookes.

Shonkoff, J. P., Hauser-Cram, P., Krauss, M. W., & Upshur, C. C. (1992). Development of infants with disabilities and their families: Implications for theory and service delivery [Special issue]. *Monographs of the Society for Research and Child Development, 57*(6).

Sloper, P., Greco, V., Beecham, J., & Webb, R. (2006). Key worker services for disabled children: What characteristics of services lead to better outcomes for children and families? *Child: Care, Health & Development, 32,* 147–157. doi:10.1111/j.1365-2214.2006.00592.x

Soukakou, E. P. (2012). Measuring quality in inclusive preschool classrooms: Development and validation of the Inclusive Classroom Profile (ICP). *Early Childhood Research Quarterly, 27,* 478–488. doi:10.1016/j.ecresq.2011.12.003

U.S. Departments of Education & Health and Human Services. (2017, January 19). *Collaboration and coordination of the Maternal, Infant, and Early Childhood Home Visiting program and the Individuals With Disabilities Education Act Part C programs.* Retrieved from https://sites.ed.gov/idea/files/ed-hhs-miechv-partc-guidance.pdf

U.S. Departments of Health and Human Services & Education. (2015, September 14). *Policy statement on inclusion of young children with disabilities in early childhood programs.* Retrieved from https://www2.ed.gov/policy/speced/guid/earlylearning/joint-statement-full-text.pdf

West, M. A., Brodbeck, F. C., & Richter, A. W. (2004). Does the 'romance of teams' exist? The effectiveness of teams in experimental and field settings. *Journal of Occupational and Organizational Psychology, 77,* 467–473. doi:10.1348/0963179042596450

Teaming and Collaboration

Educational programs and services for young children who have or are at risk for developmental delays and disabilities, by their nature, always involve more than one adult. The quality of the relationships and interactions among these adults affects the success of these programs. Teaming and collaboration practices are those that promote and sustain collaborative adult partnerships, relationships, and ongoing interactions to ensure that programs and services achieve desired child and family outcomes and goals.

It is a given that the family is an essential member of the team and that the team includes practitioners from multiple disciplines as needed. The teaming and collaboration practices we present include strategies for interacting and sharing knowledge and expertise in ways that are respectful, supportive, enhance capacity, and are culturally sensitive.

We recommend the following practices to support teaming and collaboration:

TC1. Practitioners representing multiple disciplines and families work together as a team to plan and implement supports and services to meet the unique needs of each child and family.

TC2. Practitioners and families work together as a team to systematically and regularly exchange expertise, knowledge, and information to build team capacity and jointly solve problems, plan, and implement interventions.

TC3. Practitioners use communication and group facilitation strategies to enhance team functioning and interpersonal relationships with and among team members.

TC4. Team members assist each other to discover and access community-based services and other informal and formal resources to meet family-identified child or family needs.

TC5. Practitioners and families may collaborate with each other to identify one practitioner from the team who serves as the primary liaison between the family and other team members based on child and family priorities and needs.

For Your Reference

The Teaming and Collaboration recommended practices are presented here as a reference while you read these articles. We encourage you to access the entire set of DEC Recommended Practices at …

www.dec-sped.org/dec-recommended-practices

Collaboration in Early Intervention
Teaming to Improve Outcomes for Young Children With Disabilities

Rebecca G. Lieberman-Betz
Sarah D. Wiegand
Jennifer A. Brown
Cynthia O. Vail
University of Georgia

Early one morning, Heather hopped in her pickup and headed down the forested, dirt road of her home toward the main highway into town. Heather was a physical therapist in early intervention (EI) on her way to her first home visit of the day. Heather's early intervention team had worked together for many years and included an early interventionist, speech language pathologist (SLP), occupational therapist (OT), physical therapist (PT), and nurse practitioner (NP). They worked as a cohesive unit, complemented one another's skills, and respected each other's knowledge and expertise. Their collaborative relationship did not happen overnight and took work to maintain; however, it allowed them to deliver effective services to young children and their families in their low-resourced rural community.

It is widely recognized in the field of early intervention/early childhood special education (EI/ECSE) that no individual has all the necessary knowledge and skills to serve children with disabilities and their families. As expressed in TC1, practitioners are expected to work with a team of individuals from multiple disciplines, including family members, drawing on the expertise of many to best meet the individual needs of the young children with whom they work (Chen, Klein, & Minor, 2009). There is increased awareness in the field that successful collaboration requires use of a specific skill set and strategies to support the teaming process (Bruder & Dunst, 2005). Such awareness is reflected in calls for preparation programs that focus on supporting the development of interdisciplinary and collaborative skills in practitioners entering fields where they will work with young children with disabilities (e.g., EI/ECSE, speech-language pathology, occupational therapy, physical therapy; see article by Kilgo in this monograph). In addition to the benefits of successful teaming and collaboration, challenges exist, including those posed by communication barriers and working with individuals from a variety of professional and personal backgrounds. This article aims to describe teaming and collaboration processes, discuss challenges faced when working as part of a team, and provide strategies to engage in successful teaming and collaboration when working with young children with disabilities and their families.

Defining Teaming and Collaboration

Different team approaches may be used when working with young children with disabilities. Professionals making up multidisciplinary teams operate independently, collaborating to share information rather than to shape their assessment and intervention processes. Additionally, professionals focus solely on the outcomes within their area of expertise, including intervention planning and data collection for individual outcomes. This can lead to inconsistent, disconnected services for the child and family. Professionals on interdisciplinary teams conduct assessments independently but plan for intervention more collaboratively than multidisciplinary teams. While this model incorporates more teaming than the multidisciplinary model, it still can lead to mixed messages from professionals and less continuity within services (Boyer & Thompson, 2014; Stepans, Thompson, & Buchanan, 2002).

In contrast, the transdisciplinary model necessitates team members step out from the typical boundaries of their role to provide a more holistic approach for children and families, thus requiring an immense amount of collaboration and team building (Boyer & Thompson, 2014; King et al., 2009). The primary service provider approach (PSP), a model of transdisciplinary teaming, involves collaboration among team members throughout assessment and intervention, and it is considered best practice in early intervention (Bruder, 2010). The PSP approach typically involves one provider primarily working with the child and family, who is given support and input from other team members on a regular basis (Boyer & Thompson, 2014; McWilliam, 2003).

Collaboration in the transdisciplinary model must go beyond simple teaming to build the skills of each member within and outside their specific discipline through a series of steps (King et al., 2009). Shelden and Rush (2013) outline the six steps of transdisciplinary team development as first developed by Haynes (1976) and Woodruff and McGonigel (1988). The initial step in this process is role extension, which involves members of the team partaking in professional development within their respective roles to expand their discipline specific knowledge. Role enrichment occurs when team members learn more about other team members' disciplines, leading into role expansion, which involves team members applying their acquired knowledge outside their discipline. Role exchange requires team members to embed their new skills into practice alongside their team members. This leads to role release, which is an essential feature of the transdisciplinary model and involves team members independently carrying out intervention techniques outside their role to fully support the family.

Collaboration helps to build trusting relationships with a family, especially when one team member is designated as the primary service provider.

However, *independent* may be a misleading word because a transdisciplinary team is constantly collaborating to provide the family and PSP with the appropriate support. When team members need assistance, role support is used to teach new or unfamiliar strategies to the PSP.

The morning air was chilly as Heather drove into the apartment complex of Rachel and Sara Hendricks. Sara was a beautiful little girl with shiny long hair and was always dressed in ruffled clothes containing some combination of ribbons and bows. Heather had been a member of the family's early intervention team since Sara was diagnosed with a severe seizure disorder and cerebral palsy (CP) as an infant. Because the initial priorities of the family were supporting gross motor function, it was decided that Heather, the PT, was the most appropriate primary liaison between the family and the rest of the team (TC5). Recently, however, family concerns have shifted to feeding. Because of Sara's low tone and CP, she was aspirating pureed foods and liquids. The team had been working with Rachel to orally feed her daughter safely. Several concerns persisted, including repeated aspiration, risk of lung infections, and inadequate weight gain. After a swallow study and consultation with medical professionals, a g-tube was recommended. The

team was now faced with deciding whether it was a logical time to switch the primary provider from Heather, the PT, to perhaps the OT or SLP to assist more with feeding.

Reasons and Support for Collaboration in Early Intervention

There are many reasons collaboration among team members is essential in EI. Performing assessments and writing outcomes cohesively helps with team alignment and shared goals for the child. Collaboration helps to build trusting relationships with a family, especially when one team member is designated as the PSP. This minimizes the possibility of stress and confusion resulting from a family receiving conflicting guidance from multiple providers. Through thoughtful collaboration, team members can increase efficiency and avoid holes or overlaps in service (Shelden & Rush, 2013). Team development and collaboration gives the PSP the tools he or she needs to offer the family effective intervention. Joint visits with an additional team member help provide the PSP and family with additional knowledge and resources. Frequent team meetings help to effectively plan for

Figure 1
Promoting Communication for Collaborative Teaming

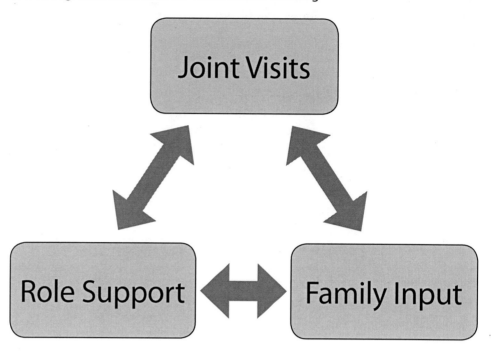

When a primary service provider (PSP) needs assistance (resulting from caregiver request, teaming discussion, and/or PSP request), consider:

- Joint visits with another team member.
- Role support through increased information sharing and problem-solving.
- Family preferences and responses.

Through this process, the provider and family team members can decide whether to maintain or switch PSPs.

intervention sessions and provide team members with support and coaching (Shelden & Rush, 2013).

As reflected in TC5 and exemplified in the vignette, a key aspect of using family priorities to drive service delivery involves collaborating closely with the family to choose a PSP whose skill set is best suited to meet the current priorities and needs of the child and family. Sheldon and Rush (2013) recommend changing PSPs as few times as possible, noting that a change in IFSP goals does not necessarily necessitate changing the PSP. However, there are times when changing the PSP will be necessary as family concerns and child needs shift (see Figure 1). Continuous assessments in EI help to ensure child and family needs remain the priority and focus of the EI team. This includes informal assessment in the form of checking in and listening to family concerns. A strong relationship between a service provider and family is imperative because it results in an open line of communication. In addition to ongoing assessment, frequent, productive team meetings can facilitate conversations that may result in the decision to change providers. Good decisions are made through thoughtful and intentional collaboration, highlighting the importance of a cohesive team in EI.

The EI team members had worked with this family for more than two years and genuinely cared for Rachel and Sara. In addition to Sara's challenges, the family had additional needs. Rachel was a young mother and also had a seizure disorder that could be controlled through medication. However, the medication did have side effects that sometimes had an impact on Rachel's functioning. Although loving, Sara's father was in and out of the home. The family was not financially stable because of Rachel's difficulties in maintaining a job and expenses related to Sara's care, and Rachel and Sara spent much of their time alone at home because of the lack of transportation and mobility equipment for Sara. This family was clearly complex in its need for various support services, which were not always readily available in the small, rural town where this family lived. The EI professionals worked together closely to support Rachel and Sara across multiple areas of need (TC1).

Collaboration and Diversity

Because of the diverse population of young children and families in the United States, it is important that service providers demonstrate competence in collaborating with others who may not share the same language or cultural background, socioeconomic status (SES), sexual orientation, gender identity, age, or family structure. As exemplified in the vignette, providers may work with parents with disabilities, those with few resources, or those who have an inconsistent family structure. Here, diversity moves beyond what may traditionally come to mind (e.g., ethnic or language diversity) but still may tap into long-held beliefs or unconscious biases that could affect providers' abilities to collaborate effectively with families. Because collaboration requires a sense of equality and mutual goals (Butera, Friesen, Horn, Palmer, & Vaiouli, 2016), it is important that providers recognize the personal biases that may emerge as a result of differences in their background, values, and life experiences compared with the families with whom they work.

Strategies to Support Collaboration With Diverse Families

It is important that providers develop and use strategies that support teaming and collaboration with diverse families and professionals. One way to recognize and actively address bias in order to establish and maintain effective collaborative relationships is through the development of cultural responsiveness. The lifelong, ongoing process of developing and maintaining cultural responsiveness will assist providers in addressing potential biases that may arise when working with individuals from different cultural backgrounds. Strategies to work toward becoming a culturally responsive provider have been described in detail by Lynch and Hanson (2011) and include developing cultural self-awareness and an understanding of the cultures of the families with whom we work. Lynch and Hanson also discuss the importance of becoming aware of how diversity across other sociocultural factors such as SES, education level, and self-efficacy beliefs may impact our interactions with others. Characteristics of providers that may

> "A key aspect of using family priorities to drive service delivery involves collaborating closely with the family to choose a PSP whose skill set is best suited to meet the current priorities and needs of the child and family.

Table 1
Strategies to Support Teaming and Collaboration With Diverse Families

1. Consider families' feelings about home visits	If families are uncomfortable meeting in their home because of living or housing conditions, suggest other locations such as a community center, the library, or other public space that is comfortable for the family.
2. Know about resources and agency contacts in the community	Identify the agencies that support families in the community along with names of agency contacts.
3. Gain knowledge and understanding of families' communities through a community mapping process	Engage in the reflective process of community mapping as described by Ordoñez-Jasis and Myck-Wayne (2012) to learn about resources in the family's community through activities such as information gathering, exploration of the community through walking or driving the area, interviews of community members to learn their point of view about resources, and reflective writing of new information gained and each family's access to resources.
4. Conduct collaborative meetings with families	Make time on a regular basis to ascertain family priorities, needs, and goals for their child and family.

support communication with others from diverse backgrounds include (a) respect for those from different cultures, (b) engagement in processes to support understanding of others' worldviews, (c) flexibility and willingness to learn, and (d) a sense of humor and ability to deal with uncertainty (Lynch & Hanson, 2011).

In addition to a personal growth process, such as development of cultural responsiveness, it is important that providers use specific strategies with families from diverse backgrounds to support effective teaming and collaboration. These strategies include considering families' feelings about home visits, identifying resources and agency contacts in the community (Derman-Sparks, Amihault, Baba, Seer, & Thompson, 2009), gaining knowledge and understanding of families' communities through a community mapping process (Ordoñez-Jasis & Myck-Wayne, 2012), and conducting collaborative meetings with families to ascertain their priorities, needs, and goals for their child and family (Banks, Santos, & Roof, 2003; see Table 1).

Communication for Collaboration

Heather's primary goal for today's home visit was to check in with the family to see how things had gone since they first discussed the g-tube as a team at a joint home visit with the OT and SLP the week before. Rachel had previously described feeding Sara as a very loving act, which supported positive interactions between mother and daughter. It enhanced Rachel's confidence in her parenting and was meaningful to the family. Rachel's initial response to the doctor's recommendation was that she did not want the g-tube placed because she feared losing this cherished activity with her daughter. The team had agreed that Rachel would talk with Sara's father and her parents about the decision and take the week to consider all options. When Heather arrived for today's home visit, Sara was sleeping peacefully in Rachel's arms, and Heather felt her heart go out to this family.

Rachel started the conversation by telling Heather about the progress Sara was making in her play and communication. Rachel had found a light-up music toy that captured Sara's attention, and that past week Sara opened and closed her fingers and looked to Rachel to indicate she wanted more of the toy. As Sara slept in her arms, Rachel showed a video of the interaction to Heather, who encouraged Rachel to share the video with the other team members through a secure video-sharing app the team used to share progress (TC3).

Heather then spent some time brainstorming with Rachel about other toys or social games that could be used to practice communication and play. Rachel then shifted the conversation to discuss the options for Sara's feeding. She and her family agreed that first and foremost they needed to ensure Sara was getting the nutrition she needed to grow and stay healthy. In effect, they had decided to go ahead and have the g-tube placed. However, Rachel wanted to continue with an oral feeding program that could be done safely because of the closeness it made her feel to Sara and because Rachel's goal was to someday wean Sara off the g-tube. Heather indicated she would be supportive of the family's decision and that there was a team of professionals available to help with this family outcome.

Communicating with provider and family team members is paramount to successful collaborative service delivery. Team members can make joint decisions and share responsibility through open and responsive communication (Coufal & Woods, 2018). Providers' unique discipline-specific knowledge and experiences, as well as families' priorities and child- and family-specific experiences, are needed for promoting child progress across developmental domains as part of comprehensive service delivery.

Therefore, as emphasized in TC3, using mutually agreed-upon, effective communication approaches underlies the success for collaborative early intervention teaming. Promoting communication for collaboration can be categorized into four components: sharing information, problem-solving, communication systems, and reflection and evaluation. Strategies and considerations for each component are provided in Table 2.

When providers share information with jargon-free explanations and discuss evidence and best practices in a family-centered individualized approach, they are increasing the family's capacity to make informed decisions. Active problem-solving approaches provide a framework for provider and family team members to make decisions about which outcomes to prioritize, which provider will act in which role, and which evidence-based strategies should be embedded in family-identified routines and activities. When a challenge arises (e.g., parent and provider don't see something the same way, child outcome progress is slow), this same problem-solving approach can be used to address the concern.

One of the first decisions that a team needs to make is how to communicate with one another. All collaborative services rely on regular informed

> **"**
>
> When providers share information with jargon-free explanations and discuss evidence and best practices in a family-centered individualized approach, they are increasing the family's capacity to make informed decisions.

Table 2
Promoting Communication for Collaborative Teaming

Communicating for collaboration	Strategies and considerations
Sharing information	• Limit jargon • Explain research evidence and best practices in a relatable and relevant way • Listen to all perspectives and offer choices/options • Use varied formats aligned with individual preferences (e.g., verbal descriptions, handouts, web resources, graphs, videos)

Problem-solving	• Make decisions as a team
	• Use a systematic problem-solving approach to arrive at decisions
	  • **Step 1:** Define the problem
	  • **Step 2:** Generate ideas
	  • **Step 3:** Evaluate ideas and decide on first action step to try
	  • **Step 4:** Develop and implement the plan

Communication systems	• Decide on mutually agreed upon ways to communicate, which may include:
	  • Face-to-face meetings
	  • Video conferencing (e.g., FaceTime, Skype, Google Hangouts)
	  • Text messaging
	  • Mobile apps for sharing messages, photos, videos, and data graphs
	  • Handwritten notes
	  • Communication notebooks
	• Discuss and define timelines and people responsible for each activity

Reflection and evaluation	• Support individual and team reflection on what is working, what can be changed, how providers and family team members are contributing
	• Evaluate team functioning and effectiveness
	  • Does the family feel as if they are provided with relevant information and receive prioritized developmental supports?
	  • Are all perspectives represented and heard?
	  • Is the child progressing toward meeting functional and meaningful outcomes?

communication, and this need is even greater with PSP approaches (Maturana, McComish, Woods, & Crais, 2011). Through the use of a problem-solving framework, the team can decide on the frequency and medium of communication. Some teams may decide to use a mobile app where text messages, videos, photos, and data can be shared. Other teams may decide on a combination of communication notebooks and monthly or every other month full team in-person meetings. Other teams may decide to have brief video conferences twice a month at the beginning of home visits. Whichever combination of options is selected, these agreed-upon systems for communication allow for team members to learn from and apply the knowledge and expertise of each person to promote child development and build family capacity. Ongoing reflection and evaluation procedures can help ensure that all perspectives are represented and provide the means to determine what's working well, what needs to be changed, and how each team member is fulfilling his or her role.

At their next team meeting, Heather shared the news of Rachel's decision with the SLP, OT, NP, and early interventionist (TC3). The family was already scheduled to have the g-tube placed, and the team had the current medical reports available. Alan, the NP, would work as the bridge between the medical team and the EI team as the family transitioned to tube feedings and a structured plan for safe oral feeding and stimulation.

Emma, the OT, and Ashley, the SLP, would work with Alan and the doctors to develop a plan to support oral feedings while Heather would remain the primary provider supporting implementation of the plan with the family. Future decisions to change the primary provider would rest on Sara's progress and Rachel's primary goals moving forward, but because mobility continued to be a high priority, and Heather had a close relationship with the family, it made sense for Heather to continue in this role (TC5).

The early interventionist would continue to consult with Heather around embedding social-communication and cognitive skills into day-to-day activities of the family and would support the family in accessing other community resources. The EI professionals felt that through collaboration, the EI team would be ready to support Sara's medical and developmental needs and the family's social needs moving forward. They also knew that because of their strong working relationships, as the child and family's needs changed, the priorities of the team would adapt to meet those needs effectively (TC1).

Conclusions

Teaming and collaboration require specific skills and use of strategies to be effective in supporting children with disabilities and their families. As illustrated in the vignette above, the use of a PSP approach (TC5) requires careful coordination with families, along with ongoing communication and collaboration across multiple disciplines to meet the unique needs of each child and family (TC1). Successful teaming and collaboration helps to enhance early intervention outcomes for children and families and should be supported through interdisciplinary personnel preparation, both preservice and in-service.

As recommended in TC3, practitioners should enhance interpersonal relationships among team members through effective communication and facilitation strategies. Agency structures such as time and paid support for team meetings, professional development, and joint home visits as well as appropriate use of technology can promote this recommended practice. Because of the unique nature of home visits, it is imperative that providers continuously examine their personal beliefs to recognize both conscious and unconscious biases. The work needed to become culturally responsive is ongoing and must be supported through professional development. Cultural responsiveness, strong communication, and collaboration skills weave together among team members to make effective early intervention teams that are ready to promote the development and well-being of infants and toddlers with disabilities and their families.

> "
>
> Ongoing reflection and evaluation procedures can help ensure that all perspectives are represented and provide the means to determine what's working well, what needs to be changed, and how each team member is fulfilling his or her role.

References

Banks, R. A., Santos, R. M., & Roof, V. (2003). Discovering family concerns, priorities, and resources: Sensitive family information gathering. *Young Exceptional Children, 6*(2), 11–19. doi:10.1177/109625060300600203

Boyer, V. E., & Thompson, S. D. (2014). Transdisciplinary model and early intervention: Building collaborative relationships. *Young Exceptional Children, 17*(3), 19–32, doi:10.1177/1096250613493446

Bruder, M. B. (2010). Early childhood intervention: A promise to children and families for their future. *Exceptional Children, 76*, 339–355. doi:10.1177/001440291007600306

Bruder, M. B., & Dunst, C. J. (2005). Personnel preparation in recommended early intervention practices: Degree of emphasis across disciplines. *Topics in Early Childhood Special Education, 25*, 25–33. doi:10.1177/02711214050250010301

Butera, G. D., Friesen, A., Horn, E. M., Palmer, S. B., & Vaiouli, P. (2016). Adults working and playing well together. In E. M. Horn, S. B. Palmer, G. D. Butera, & J. A. Lieber (Eds.), *Six steps to inclusive preschool curriculum: A UDL-based framework for children's school success* (pp. 183–196). Baltimore, MD: Paul H. Brookes.

Chen, D., Klein, M. D., & Minor, L. (2009). Interdisciplinary perspectives in early intervention: Professional development in multiple disabilities through distance education. *Infants & Young Children, 22*, 146–158. doi:10.1097/IYC.ob013e3181a030e0

Coufal, K. L., & Woods, J. J. (2018). Interprofessional collaborative practice in early intervention. *Pediatric Clinics of North America, 65*, 143–155. doi:10.1016/j.pcl.2017.08.027

Derman-Sparks, L., Amihault, C., Baba, S., Seer, N., & Thompson, S. (2009). Children—socioeconomic class and equity. *Young Children, 64*(3), 50–53.

Haynes, U. (1976). The UCP National Collaborative Infant Project. In T. D. Tjossem (Ed.), *Intervention strategies for high-risk infants and young children* (pp. 509–534). Baltimore, MD: University Park Press.

King, G., Strachan, D., Tucker, M., Duwyn, B., Desserud, S., & Shillington, M. (2009). The application of a transdisciplinary model for early intervention services. *Infants & Young Children, 22*, 211–223. doi:10.1097/IYC.ob013e3181abe1c3

Lynch, E. W., & Hanson, M. J. (Eds.). (2011). *Developing cross-cultural competence: A guide for working with children and their families* (4th ed.). Baltimore, MD: Paul H. Brookes.

Marturana, E., McComish, C., Woods, J., & Crais, E. (2011). Early intervention teaming and the primary service provider approach: Who does what, when, why, and how? *SIG 1 Perspectives on Language Learning and Education, 18*(2), 47–52. doi:10.1044/lle18.2.47

McWilliam, R. A. (2003). The primary-service-provider model for home- and community-based services. *Psicologia, 17*(1), 115–135.

Ordoñez-Jasis, R., & Myck-Wayne, J. (2012). Community mapping in action: Uncovering resources and assets for young children and their families. *Young Exceptional Children, 15*(3), 31–45. doi:10.1177/1096250612451756

Shelden, M. L., & Rush, D. D. (2013). *The early intervention teaming handbook: The primary service provider approach.* Baltimore, MD: Paul H. Brookes.

Stepans, M., Thompson, C. L., & Buchanan, M. L. (2002). The role of the nurse on a transdisciplinary early intervention assessment team. *Public Health Nursing, 19,* 238–245. doi:10.1046/j.1525-1446.2002.19403.x

Woodruff, G., & McGonigel, M. J. (1988). Early intervention team approaches: The transdisciplinary model. In J. B. Jordan, J. J. Gallagher, P. L. Hutinger, & M. B. Karnes (Eds.), *Early childhood special education: Birth to three* (pp. 163–181). Reston, VA: Council for Exceptional Children.

2

Using Technology to Support Teaming With Families That Are Culturally and Linguistically Diverse

Sara E. Luke
Mercer University

Isabela Montoya is a 3-year-old girl with an autism spectrum disorder. After transitioning from early intervention, she will attend an inclusive preschool class-room, Little Kids Preschool (LKP). This classroom has 15 students, five of whom have special needs of varying degrees, and two teachers, one special education teacher and one general education teacher. While in early intervention, Isabella received speech therapy for 30 minutes twice a week along with one hour per week of occupational therapy in her home. Isabela was evaluated by the local public school system evaluation team, and she qualified for special education services in an inclusive preschool classroom for six hours per day, along with two hours of speech therapy per week. Her mother, Natalia, has requested that Isabela attend LKP because the preschool has several staff members who speak both English and Spanish. Natalia's first language is Spanish, and she is still learning English. She feels more comfortable having adults in her daughter's school whom she can turn to for communication assistance, if needed.

Natalia had developed a warm relationship with Isabela's early intervention family coordinator, Alexa, and felt comfortable expressing her opinions and offering her observations about Isabela's development. Although Alexa spoke English at their monthly home visits, she always made sure an interpreter was present at formal team meetings, such as Isabela's Individualized Family Service Plan (IFSP) meetings. This allowed Natalia to use Spanish or English to communicate with the other members of the early intervention team. Now that Isabela is 3 years old and has transitioned to school-based services, Natalia wonders whether her limited ability to speak English will be a problem for her daughter's new teachers and school.

Alexa had always come to their home and worked with Isabela. Natalia never had to wonder what happened during therapies because everyone worked together. She felt like an equal part of the early intervention team because she observed the same things the other service providers observed. They discussed their observations as they occurred in her home. Now that Isabela was going to attend school each day, Natalia worried that she wouldn't get to see how the teachers and therapists worked with her daughter. She would also miss out on seeing how Isabela responded to them. She couldn't rely on Isabela to communicate what happened at school like other 3-year-old children might because of her significant communication delay.

Natalia was worried. How would she know what happened at school? What if the teachers didn't tell her everything? How would she know if Isabela liked her teachers? She would rely heavily on the teachers in Isabela's class to communicate what happened daily so that she could operate as part of her daughter's IEP team. Natalia felt uneasy about being a member of this "IEP" team, and she wondered how she was going to participate on a team when she wasn't even sure what "IEP" meant?

The Individuals With Disabilities Educational Improvement Act (IDEA) of 2004 mandates that parents and schools work together to develop an Individualized Education Program (IEP) for children (3–21 years old) with disabilities. A child's IEP includes elements such as evaluation and eligibility, goal identification, behavior support plans, assistive technology, and related services. IEPs are legal contracts between parents and schools that outline the specific measurable goals and the services needed to educate children with special needs.

IEP teams are composed of a variety of different disciplines, depending on the needs of individual children, and may include speech therapists, occupational therapists, physical therapists, nurses, administrators, and social workers. Families are also clearly team members (Division for Early Childhood [DEC], 2014; IDEA, 2004), and family-centered practices are a cornerstone of the field of early childhood special education (Copple & Bredekamp, 2009). IDEA (2004) identifies specific provisions for this collaboration between parents and schools, including notification of meetings with mutually agreed-upon meeting locations and times in the parents' primary language, a written copy of parents' rights, an interpreter for parents with limited English proficiency, and information regarding what the meeting is about and who will be in attendance.

IDEA (2004) states that parents have the right to be "full and equal participants" in their children's IEP meetings and services (34 CFR 300.322). The work of the IEP team could be compromised if schools and practitioners view having parents at IEP meetings as a legal requirement rather than seeing parents as team members to confer and collaborate with on a regular basis. Interdisciplinary collaboration and teaming are essential for designing, implementing, and evaluating special education services for young children from a variety of services providers. Input from different disciplines, as well as the parents and families of the young children receiving the services, is essential (McWilliam, 2005). In essence, IEP teaming should be viewed as a series of ongoing interactions among all members that result in shared knowledge, problem-solving, and decision-making

> IEP teaming should be viewed as a series of ongoing interactions among all members that result in shared knowledge, problem-solving, and decision-making rather than just a single meeting people attend for delivering information.

rather than just a single meeting people attend for delivering information. While schools are legally required to meet the IDEA mandates about collaborating with families, the mandates themselves merely secure parents' *attendance* at IEP meetings and not their *participation* as a member of their children's IEP team (Wolfe & Durán, 2013).

Teaming and collaboration are synonymous with teaching young children who have disabilities or are at risk for them because multiple adults from various disciplines often provide their services. Collaboration among multiple team members from different disciplines can be a challenge, and despite the plethora of research on collaboration between families and schools in general (Blue-Banning, Summers, Frankland, Nelson, & Beegle, 2004; Cheatham, Hart, Malian, & McDonald, 2012; Haines, 2015; Staples & Diliberto, 2010), families of young children with disabilities still express displeasure with their experiences on their children's IEP teams (Resch et al., 2010; Slade, Eisenhower, Carter, & Blacher, 2018). Families that are culturally and linguistically diverse may experience even

more difficulties when interacting with their children's special education service providers and schools (Fults & Harry, 2012; Rossetti et al., 2018).

Families that are culturally and linguistically diverse have identified several interpersonal factors that negatively impact their perceptions and experiences with teaming or collaborating with schools. These include, but are not limited to, a lack of respect, being misunderstood, an absence of cultural responsiveness, unsuitable language accommodations, and negative perspectives of families and children by professionals (Lo, 2012; Wolfe & Durán, 2013). These barriers not only hinder their participation in their children's special education services as stated in IDEA, they also impact the quality and effectiveness of those services.

The Division for Early Childhood (2014) published a series of recommended practices that are meant to bridge the gap for practitioners between research and classroom practices. This article focuses on two teaming strategies (TC2 and TC3) in hopes that practitioners see the importance of families' authentic participation on their children's IEP teams and implement these strategies in innovative and culturally responsive ways that embrace the uniqueness of children with special needs and their families.

TC2 encourages practitioners to "systematically and regularly exchange information" (DEC, 2014, p. 15) so the team can solve problems, plan, and work together to achieve better service provision for children. One way practitioners might incorporate this practice into their classrooms is by meeting with all team members in an informal setting to develop a team communication

Figure 1
Isabela's Team Communication Plan (TCP)

Child's Name: Isabela Montoya   **Date of Plan:** 9-2-2018
DOB: 9-01-2015 (3 years old)

Team members roles and responsibilities

Name	Role	Communication schedule	Format	Language	Technology
Ms. Jody	Preschool special education teacher	Daily/weekly	Conversations/ posts to ClassDojo	English	ClassDojo
Ms. Jill	Speech therapist	Weekly	Posts to ClassDojo	English	ClassDojo
Ms. Ana	General education preschool teacher	Daily/weekly	Posts to ClassDojo	English	ClassDojo
Natalia	Isabela's mother	Daily/weekly	Conversations/ posts to ClassDojo	English and Spanish	ClassDojo

TCP monitor: Ms. Jody will consult with each team member at least every nine weeks and solicit feedback regarding the effectiveness of the TCP. Team members' feedback will be documented in the boxes below. Changes will be made as needed based on feedback.

Team Members	First 9 weeks	Second 9 weeks	Third 9 weeks	Fourth 9 weeks
Jody				
Jill				
Ana				
Natalia				

Formal meeting considerations: Interpreter needed at all formal meetings (not yet scheduled).

Language considerations: Spanish and English spoken in the home. Natalia (mother) is currently learning English. Team will use ClassDojo app to communicate on daily/weekly basis.

Notes:

plan for exchanging information with one another (see Figure 1 for a completed communication plan for Isabela). Students' case managers or classroom teachers should initiate the development of the plan and monitor its effectiveness. For example, a teacher may informally evaluate the communication plan by individually speaking with different team members quarterly and making changes as needed.

Team members should discuss the frequency, composition, detail, and format (i.e., paper, digital, audio) of the communication plan. They might also establish a schedule for corresponding, such as daily, weekly, or monthly. It may be that some team members are scheduled less frequently than others because of the nature of their service provision (e.g., a nurse may consult once a month and only provide monthly updates). The language used in the communication plan is also important. It can also be helpful to ask culturally responsive questions such as: Do all team members use the same language to communicate? Do all team members read in the same language? What are the team members preferred means of receiving and giving communication? (Rossetti, Sauer, Bui, & Ou, 2017)

Both Isabela's special education teacher and general education teacher met with Natalia and Alexa a few days before Isabela started at LKP to set up a team communication plan that would support their regular communication. Isabela's speech therapist attended the meeting via FaceTime. When Isabela's special education teacher scheduled the meeting with Natalia, she suggested Natalia invite Alexa to join them at the meeting. The special education teacher hoped that having two of the primary members of Isabela's former early intervention team at the meeting would help build a bridge to the new team by offering background information, strategies, and anything else pertinent for building Isabela's new IEP team's capacity.

The transition from early intervention services to preschool special education services is significant for families as the services change from home-based (Part C) with a family focus to school-based (Part B) with a child focus (IDEA, 2004). In Natalia's case, she is unsure of how she will function in her role as a member of her daughter's new IEP team because the service models and team roles will be considerably different. Prior team dynamics and experiences in early intervention may impact families' expectations for teaming in preschool special education services (Podvey, Hinojosa, & Koenig, 2013). Isabela's special education teacher invited Natalia to bring Isabela's early intervention family coordinator with her to the new team meeting to help create a smoother transition from Part C to Part B services. Alexa's participation could help provide the new team with information about the roles and routines of the early intervention team and provide Natalia with support when meeting the new service providers (e.g., teachers, therapists, administrators). Preschool special education practitioners can also benefit from including early intervention providers in initial team meetings because this may help with the transition process and team building.

At the meeting, the five women discussed some of the strategies the former early intervention team members had used to communicate with one another. Natalia

> "
>
> Team members should discuss the frequency, composition, detail, and format (i.e., paper, digital, audio) of the communication plan. They might also establish a schedule for corresponding.

and Alexa mentioned the words "conversations" and "observations" frequently when they described the early intervention team's communication. Ms. Jody, the special education teacher, surmised that those two things would be important to include and incorporate into the IEP team's communication plan. After a 10-minute discussion, team members decided they needed to establish a routine communication schedule. They also identified the need for a documentation system that provided all team members with similar information about Isabela's progress on goals and objectives.

The documentation system would be important because different professionals would support Isabela throughout the school day and in different contexts. Furthermore, her mother would not be observing her during the day, and the other professionals would not be observing Isabela at home in the afternoons. They agreed that weekly information regarding Isabela's goals and objectives should be shared informally through conversations and that monthly discussions summarizing Isabela's progress on goals and objectives would take place via phone

or in person. Ms. Jody also added that because Natalia preferred the use of a translator at formal meetings, one would be present during all formal meetings at school. Natalia and Alexa looked at one another and smiled. This meeting was off to a great start.

When working with families that are culturally and linguistically diverse, one factor practitioners must consider is language translation during formal meetings. Hart, Cheatham, and Jimenez-Silva (2012) emphasized the need for IEP teams to provide quality translation services to families that are culturally and linguistically diverse. If quality translation does not occur, families may not be able to participate as full and active team members; therefore, the quality of translation during formal meetings is a determining factor in successful teaming. Isabela's team addressed the issue of translation and planned when and how the translation services would occur based on her mother's needs and preferences.

During the meeting, Isabela's special education teacher listened very carefully as Natalia and the early intervention family coordinator, Alexa, explained the former communication routine. Involving all team members in creating a communication routine and considering the utility of a previous team's system for communication are useful strategies.

The routines and procedures of the former team provided valuable input for the new team regarding what worked or did not work as well as what the family might expect from new team members. This will also allow teams to problem-solve any current issues and improve upon the previous plan if needed. Developing a team communication plan is one example of how practitioners can incorporate TC2: regular communication among team members.

Along with using systematic communication to work together to problem-solve and implement services, practitioners might also consider using strategies to build relationships with and share knowledge with one another. TC3 encourages practitioners to "use communication and group facilitation strategies to enhance team functioning and interpersonal relationships with and among team members" (DEC, 2014, p. 15). Teachers implementing this practice might use technology to enhance their teams' daily functioning and interactions with one another. Technology can increase communication among team members because of the access and convenience it provides, especially for families not available during school hours (Vismara, Young, & Rogers, 2012). For example, a teacher might take a video of a child performing a task and e-mail or text it to a parent's mobile device. That parent can then view the video and respond when it is convenient for him or her.

Another way practitioners could implement TC3 in formal settings is to support their teams in establishing communication norms for team meetings such as IEP meetings and conferences. These norms could be developed by the teams at the initial meeting and would be the "rules of communication" at team meetings. Some examples of norms might include: everyone listens while one person speaks, one team member writes questions down on note cards and puts them in the center of the table for end-of-meeting review, the team uses a round robin format for speaking, etc. This group facilitation strategy could help ensure all team members are actively participating at formal meetings.

As the meeting progressed, Natalia expressed concern about not knowing what happened during the school day with Isabela. She reiterated that she felt like an equal part of the early intervention team because she observed the same things the other service providers observed and those observations were discussed as they occurred in her home. She added that she was worried about not being able to see Isabela's functioning at school and that she needed to see what the teachers and therapists saw so she could know what was going on. Alexa added that Natalia was concerned about knowing what the teachers saw so she could make informed decisions along with Isabela's other IEP team members. The team discussed the next aspect of their communication plan and focused on the format they might use to share information with one another.

From a practical standpoint, special education practitioners, school therapists, administrators, and other IEP team members usually have the benefit of seeing one another frequently and serving children in the same school building, often in the same classrooms. At the very least, they have the opportunity for frequent and informal conversations about how children are progressing simply because of their proximity to one another. On the other hand, families do not attend school with their children and may not have similar opportunities to generate opinions in conjunction with other professionals about their children's progress without intentional strategies in place. Practitioners must consider ways they can facilitate the sharing of children's functioning with all IEP team members, even when those members are not there in person. Slade et al. (2018) found that

> Along with using systematic communication to work together to problem-solve and implement services, practitioners might also consider using strategies to build relationships with and share knowledge with one another.

parents of young children with autism spectrum disorder expressed that regular communication and interaction with other IEP team members laid the foundation for a satisfactory and positive experience as a team member throughout the school year, as well as during annual IEP meetings.

Ms. Jill, the speech-language pathologist (SLP), suggested the team consider using a free phone app that would allow all team members to have access to Isabela's online portfolio. When Natalia heard "phone app," she was immediately interested. She used her phone frequently for day-to-day tasks and wanted to hear more about the app. The team discussed the benefits of using the app, ClassDojo. Ms. Jill explained that the app would only allow private access to Isabela's online portfolio where pictures and videos of her could be posted for other IEP team members to comment on. The team members would need a password to get access to Isabela's information, and they agreed to keep the password confidential. The team agreed that ClassDojo would support their efforts to collaborate because it would allow all team members to develop their conclusions about what they watched in a video or noted in a picture. Team members could also use the app to share videos of particular strategies they were using with Isabela that would aid other team members in using the strategies in the same manner.

Finally, the app could benefit multilingual teams because it included a translate button for users to convert typed text into a language of their choosing. For example, if her special education teacher commented on a video in the portfolio in English, Natalia could tap the translate button and read the comment in Spanish. After hearing the details of the phone app, Natalia was very excited. Each team member downloaded the app and created an online portfolio for Isabela. At the conclusion of the meeting, Natalia expressed her excitement about the upcoming school year. Her concerns about being a part of Isabela's IEP team and knowing what Isabela did daily were satisfied. She looked forward to being a part of her daughter's new team and felt her daughter's new preschool special education services were off to a good start.

As demonstrated in the example above, the use of ClassDojo, in conjunction with phone conversations, e-mails, or informal face-to-face chats, provided all IEP team members essential information about Isabela's performance in various settings. This is a good example of how Isabela's IEP team incorporated TC3 to improve its team functioning through the use of technology. Although Isabela's team decided to use ClassDojo, face-to-face meetings and conversations were not discontinued; rather, the team included the use of technology as a supplement to its scheduled conversations and formal meetings. While the use of technology can enhance collaboration among team members, it may not eliminate the need for face-to-face meetings and discussions (Riggleman & Buchter, 2017).

When choosing to use technology to support TC2 and TC3 in general, practitioners need to consider issues regarding privacy and confidentiality, practicality, and accessibility (Riggleman & Buchter, 2017). As described in Isabela's story, only team members had access to the communications (privacy), the team needed frequent communication (practicality), and all team members had a

> Although the team decided to use the ClassDojo smartphone app, face-to-face meetings and conversations were not discontinued; rather, the team included the use of technology as a supplement to its scheduled conversations and formal meetings.

mobile phone with regular Internet access (accessibility). More specifically, when working with families that are culturally and linguistically diverse, the language accessibility of the technology is also important. In Isabela's case, her mother could use a translate button in the app to read in Spanish what her teachers had typed in English. ClassDojo provided an accessible platform for all team members to communicate in their primary language. Practitioners using technology that provides access to multiple languages and not just English supports families that are culturally and linguistically diverse (Wolfe & Durán, 2013).

While the ClassDojo app was a suitable strategy for Isabela's IEP team, the use of this technology might not meet the needs of other families and other teams. Practitioners must think about factors such as families' cultures, locations, and socioeconomic resources when considering the use of technology (Riggleman & Buchter, 2017). For example, if a family does not have regular Internet access but does have mobile phone access, ClassDojo would not be an ideal choice for that team. A more suitable option for collaboration may be home visits along with group phone calls.

Another example may be a family whose culture or values do not support the use of technology; they may simply prefer to use written or spoken communication. Thus, it is important for teams to establish a communication plan when they form their teams. All team members can contribute to creating the team communication plan and decide how the team will collaborate and work together. While using technology for team collaboration may not be appropriate for all teams, it is the author's hope that teams simply consider *if* and *how* it might be used to incorporate TC2 and TC3 for teaming with families of young children with disabilities.

Overall, teaming and collaboration require effort and an inclusive perspective. Preschool practitioners can learn about and implement successful early intervention team strategies so that outcomes for families and children are equally successful in preschool. Moore et al. (2012) emphasized the need for team members to "leave your title at the door" and work willingly to support, learn from, and teach one another (p. 105).

Collaborating and teaming with all families of students, regardless of language, culture, or ability, is essential in supporting the development of young children with disabilities (Rossetti et al., 2017). If practitioners keep this in mind as they facilitate IEP teams for their young students with disabilities, work with families to regularly exchange expertise and problem-solve, and implement strategies to build interpersonal relationships, there will be better outcomes for children and their families (Bruder, 2010).

References

Blue-Banning, M., Summers, J. A., Frankland, H. C., Nelson, L. L., & Beegle, G. (2004). Dimensions of family and professional partnerships: Constructive guidelines for collaboration. *Exceptional Children, 70*, 167–184. doi:10.1177/001440290407000203

Bruder, M. B. (2010). Early childhood intervention: A promise to children and families for their future. *Exceptional Children, 76*, 339–355. doi:10.1177/001440291007600306

Cheatham, G. A., Hart, J. E., Malian, I., & McDonald, J. (2012). Six things to never say or hear during an IEP meeting: Educators as advocates for families. *Teaching Exceptional Children, 44*(3), 50–57. doi:10.1177/004005991204400306

Copple, C., & Bredekamp, S. (Eds.). (2009). *Developmentally appropriate practice in early childhood programs serving children from birth through age 8* (3rd ed.). Washington, DC: NAEYC.

Division for Early Childhood. (2014). *DEC recommended practices in early intervention/early childhood special education 2014.* Retrieved from http://www.dec-sped.org/dec-recommended-practices

Fults, R. M., & Harry, B. (2012). Combining family centeredness and diversity in early childhood teacher training programs. *Teacher Education and Special Education, 35*, 27–48. doi:10.1177/0888406411399784

Haines, S. J., Gross, J. M. S., Blue-Banning, M., Francis, G. L., & Turnbull, A. P. (2015). Fostering family-school and community-school partnerships in inclusive schools: Using practice as a guide. *Research and Practice for Persons With Severe Disabilities, 40*, 227–239. doi:10.1177/1540796915594141

Hart, J. E., Cheatham, G., & Jimenez-Silva, M. (2012). Facilitating quality language interpretation for families of diverse students with special needs. *Preventing School Failure, 56*, 207–213. doi:10.1080/1045988X.2011.645910

Individuals With Disabilities Education Act, 20 U.S.C. § 1400 (2004).

Lo, L. (2012). Demystifying the IEP process for diverse parents of children with disabilities. *Teaching Exceptional Children, 44*(3), 14–20. doi:10.1177/004005991204400302

McWilliam, R. A. (2005). DEC recommended practices: Interdisciplinary models. In S. Sandall, M. L. Hemmeter, B. J. Smith, & M. E. McLean (Eds.), *DEC recommended practices: A comprehensive guide for practical application in early intervention/early childhood special education* (pp. 127–131). Longmont, CO: Sopris West.

Moore, L., Koger, D., Blomberg, S., Legg, L., McConahy, R., Wit, S., & Gatmaitan, M. (2012). Making best practice our practice: Reflections on our journey into natural environments. *Infants & Young Children, 25*, 95–105. doi:10.1097/IYC.ob013e31823d0592

Podvey, M. C., Hinojosa, J., & Koenig, K. P. (2013). Reconsidering insider status for families during the transition from early intervention to preschool special education. *Journal of Special Education, 46*, 211–222. doi:10.1177/0022466911407074

Resch, J. A., Mireles, G., Benz, M. R., Grenwelge, C., Peterson, R., & Zhang, D. (2010). Giving parents a voice: A qualitative study of the challenges experienced by parents of children with disabilities. *Rehabilitation Psychology, 55*, 139–150. doi:10.1037/a0019473

Riggleman, S., & Buchter, J. M. (2017). Using internet-based applications to increase collaboration among stakeholders in special education. *Journal of Special Education Technology, 32*, 232–239. doi:10.1177/0162643417725882

Rossetti, Z., Redash, A., Sauer, J. S., Bui, O., Wen, Y., & Regensburger, D. (2018). Access, accountability, and advocacy: Culturally and linguistically diverse families' participation in IEP meetings. *Exceptionality*. Advance online publication. doi:10.1080/09362835.2018.1480948

Rossetti, Z., Sauer, J. S., Bui, O., & Ou, S. (2017). Developing collaborative partnerships with culturally and linguistically diverse families during the IEP process. *Teaching Exceptional Children, 49*, 328–338. doi:10.1177/0040059916680103

Slade, N., Eisenhower, A., Carter, A. S., & Blacher, J. (2018). Satisfaction with individualized education programs among parents of young children with ASD. *Exceptional Children, 84*, 242–260. doi:10.1177/0014402917742923

Staples, K. E., & Diliberto, J. A. (2010). Guidelines for successful parent involvement: Working with parents of students with disabilities. *Teaching Exceptional Children, 42*(6), 58–63. doi:10.1177/004005991004200607

Vismara, L. A., Young, G. S., & Rogers, S. J. (2012). Telehealth for expanding the reach of early autism training to parents. *Autism Research and Treatment*, Art. 121878. doi:10.1155/2012/121878

Wolfe, K., & Durán, L. K. (2013). Culturally and linguistically diverse parents' perceptions of the IEP process: A review of current research. *Multiple Voices for Ethnically Diverse Exceptional Learners, 13*(2), 4–18.

3

Collaborative Teaming Between Speech-Language Pathologists and Paraprofessionals to Improve the Language Skills of Young Children With Disabilities
A Dialogic Reading Intervention

JACQUELINE A. TOWSON
University of Central Florida

KATHERINE B. GREEN
University of West Georgia

Mrs. Davis is a prekindergarten teacher in an inclusive charter school. Her classroom consists of children of multiple abilities, with three children who receive speech and language therapy. In her classroom, Mrs. Davis has one full-time paraprofessional (Mr. Stanfield), a speech-language pathologist who provides in-class speech-language therapy twice a week (Mrs. Houze), and a special educator who provides in-class support two hours per day (Ms. Shah). For the majority of the day, it is only Mrs. Davis and Mr. Stanfield in the classroom with the children. While Mrs. Davis has received training from Mrs. Houze on evidence-based practices, such as dialogic reading, she believes that if all team members received this type of training, outcomes for the children in her class would improve. She relies on Mr. Stanfield to meet many of the children's academic needs, particularly those who need extra assistance; yet, he has not received any professional development nor educational training on meeting the academic needs of children with disabilities. The children greatly benefit from Mr. Stanfield's presence and performance in the classroom. Mrs. Davis and Mrs. Houze believe that child outcomes would improve even more if Mr. Stanfield was provided professional development on how to meet the academic needs of children with disabilities.

Speech and Language Delays in Young Children

Speech and language delays in young children typically involve significant deficits in oral language skills, specifically receptive language (the ability to understand), expressive language (the ability to express), and vocabulary (Bucholz & Green,

2018). These deficits may lead to persistent challenges in reading, writing, and emergent literacy skills as children enter elementary school (Marvin, 1994; National Institute of Child Health and Human Development Early Child Care Research Network, 2005). Addressing language delays in preschool is imperative because more than 69% of children identified as having a disability in preschool, particularly language impairments, are identified 10 years later as having a learning disability (Aram, Ekelman, & Nation, 1984). Communication and language interventions for young children with significant language impairments can be effective, particularly when the interventions occur early in life (Odom & Wolery, 2003). Thus, it is important for classroom teachers, paraprofessionals, and therapists to work together as a team to exchange expertise, knowledge, and information to implement interventions that occur within the daily routine (TC2; Carlson, Bitterman, & Jenkins, 2012; Koppenhaver, Hendrix, & Williams, 2007).

Professional Development With Paraprofessionals

There is a critical shortage of speech-language pathologists (SLPs) in the schools (American Speech-Language-Hearing Association [ASHA], 2014). A shortage of SLPs can impede the progress of children with disabilities to achieve their maximum potential, particularly in the area of language development (Schooling, 2003). Collaboration among SLPs, classroom teachers, and paraprofessionals is a viable way to extend and supplement the services provided by SLPs in the school setting (ASHA, 2010), building team capacity to be able to jointly solve problems and implement interventions (TC1, TC2). A paraprofessional (or paraeducator) is defined by Title I as "an employee of an LEA (local educational agency) who provides instructional support" (U.S. Department of Education, 2004). Paraprofessionals often educate children with disabilities in the classroom, yet they may lack sufficient training or professional development for working with students with a variety of abilities (Chopra et al., 2004; Trautman, 2004). Paraprofessionals, however, have expressed interest in professional development related specifically to service delivery (Killoran, Templeman, Peters, & Udell, 2001) because they may feel undervalued in their ability to contribute to their classrooms without sufficient training (Chopra et al., 2004; Riggs, 2001; Wallace, 2004).

There is an emerging literature base on educating paraprofessionals to implement evidence-based strategies such as peer facilitation, reading instruction, and behavioral strategies (TC1; Causton-Theoharis, & Malmgren, 2005; Cobb, 2007; Hall, Grundon, Pope, & Romero, 2010). Most recently, paraprofessionals have been trained to improve outcomes for elementary-aged children with autism by providing students with opportunities to respond and initiate, by implementing a systematic prompting hierarchy (Wermer, Brock, & Seaman, 2017), by increasing their use of prompting procedures and associated practices (Ledford, Zimmerman, Harbin, & Ward, 2017), and by improving the use of environmental arrangement, prompting, and praise in inclusive classrooms (Ledford, Zimmerman, Chazin, et al., 2017). Researchers are examining not only how to provide professional development to paraprofessionals but how to properly use paraprofessionals in special education programs (French, 2003; Hall et al., 2010). One example of a paraprofessional professional development program was conducted in Canada. The program was designed to extend SLP services to populations where services are scarce or nonexistent (Hus, 2014). Paraprofessionals in Canada were offered a series of college courses to earn a "certificate of competence in language stimulation" to address shortages of SLPs in their country (Hus, 2014). Causton-Theoharis and Malmgren (2005) also trained paraprofessionals to facilitate interactions between students with severe disabilities and their peers, with increased rates of both facilitation and student interaction. When developing training programs for paraprofessionals, important characteristics of the trainings include long-range programs and comprehensive and systematic programs (Vasa, Steckelberg, & Pickett, 2003).

Mr. Stanfield is in his third year as a prekindergarten paraprofessional. He en-

joys his position but now desires more knowledge to make a greater impact on the children in the class. He often works with the children who require additional assistance in the classroom, such as those with developmental delays. The SLP, Mrs. Houze, provides speech-language therapy within the classroom. Mr. Stanfield frequently asks Mrs. Houze how he could better support the children in the classroom. Mrs. Houze realizes that Mr. Stanfield, if given the opportunity and education, could have a great impact on the children with speech and language delays, particularly because he is in the class with them all day, whereas her time with the students is limited. Mrs. Houze sees an opportunity to further enhance her reach into the classroom by having Mr. Stanfield support the children's language development during the day.

Collaboration Using an Appreciative Inquiry Approach

The Division for Early Childhood (DEC, 2014) and ASHA (2010) recommend that practitioners who represent multiple disciplines and families work together as a team to plan and implement supports and services to meet the unique needs of each child and family (TC1). A multidisciplinary collaboration among special education teachers, paraprofessionals, and SLPs allows for sharing of expertise among different professionals and better supports outcomes for all children in the classroom and their families (TC2; Idol, Nevin, & Paolucci-Whitcomb, 2000; Pugach, Blanton, Correa, McLeskey, & Langley, 2009). Collaboration, as defined by Schrage (1995), is "the process of *shared creation*: two or more individuals with complementary skills interacting to create a shared understanding that none had previously possessed or could have come to on their own" (p. 29). There is preliminary evidence for improved student outcomes in elementary school when collaborative opportunities are provided for professionals in educational settings; however, there is limited guidance on how to define and measure effective collaboration (Goddard, Goddard, & Tschannen-Moran, 2007). When educational professionals collaborate, opportunities arise to problem solve, tailor instruction to students, and build knowledge-creating learning communities (Pugach et al., 2009). To form an effective collaboration, professionals benefit from identifying a specific problem, analyzing factors that contribute to the problem, developing feasible interventions, implementing strategies, and evaluating the effectiveness of those implemented strategies (TC2; Allen & Graden, 2002).

Appreciative inquiry (AI) is a successful approach to collaboration in school settings (Calabrese, Hester, Friesen, & Burkhalter, 2010; Dickerson & Helm-Stevens, 2011). AI, grounded in social constructivism (Watkins, Mohr, & Kelly, 2011), is a method of collaboration that uses a strength-based model of change (Cooperrider & Whitney, 2005; Filleul & Rowland, 2006). In particular, the AI process creates change by capitalizing on positive emotions, finding others'

strengths, and building relationships, as opposed to finding others' weaknesses or using a deficit approach (Waters & White, 2015). When using AI, professionals create change by using positive language and collective inquiry to lead the team to the ideal future. Thus, AI, using the power of positivity and communication, can lead to greater collaboration among professionals. For example, when given a new project or idea, the professionals will work together to cocreate and codesign the ideal project by focusing on positives of the current state of the situation (i.e., "the best of what is") and positive communication (Dickerson & Helm-Stevens, 2011).

There are five phases in AI: definition, discovery, dream, design, and destiny (Watkins et al., 2011). Within the definition phase, critical beginning questions are asked, such as the participation and roles of the team members as well as the project goals. The discovery phase encourages team members to notice and appreciate the current processes when everything is running in optimal conditions. The dream phase allows team members to discuss and share what their dreams would be in the classroom—whether those dreams were the norm, and not the exception. The design phase is when the team members cocreate or design the processes or program to get to the dream or ideal classroom. Finally, the destiny phase is when the design and the dream are implemented.

It is recommended that practitioners use communication facilitation strategies to enhance team functioning and interpersonal relationships with and among team members (TC3; DEC, 2014). Professionals may consider using an AI approach when collaborating (Cooperrider, Whitney, & Stavros, 2008) because

AI can enhance communication among team members by promoting shared strengths and assets as well as building relationships among school personnel (Calabrese et al., 2010). For example, rather than the SLP providing consultative training to a paraprofessional, AI will help facilitate a collaborative partnership.

Mrs. Houze observed Mr. Stanfield's interactions with the children who received speech-language therapy. She observed that Mr. Stanfield read storybooks to small groups of children during center time and noticed the excitement in his voice and the children's attention to the story. The children were praised when sitting criss-cross, listening, and not interrupting the story. Mr. Stanfield asked very few questions, and the children did not interact with the story. Mrs. Houze noticed several missed opportunities to enhance the children's language skills. After reflecting, Mrs. Houze recognized an opportunity to collaborate with Mr. Stanfield around dialogic reading to enhance language instruction in the classroom.

Dialogic Reading

Dialogic reading (DR) is an evidence-based practice to increase children's expressive vocabulary and oral language skills, specifically children who are at-risk (What Works Clearinghouse, 2007), with emerging evidence for children with disabilities (Fleury, Miramontez, Hudson, & Schwartz, 2014; Towson, Gallagher, & Bingham, 2016). Through DR, the adult facilitates the child's increased verbal participation through two sets of strategies, one related to the types of prompts (or questions) for the adult to present and the second implemented to scaffold increased language use (Lonigan & Whitehurst, 1998). First, DR incorporates five types of prompts implemented by adults while reading picture books with children, referred to by the acronym CROWD (i.e., completion, recall, open-ended, wh-questions, distancing). The second DR strategy is represented by the acronym PEER, in which the adult follows up on the *prompts* to *evaluate* what the child said, *expand* on that response, and provide the child an opportunity to practice the expansion by *repeating* the prompt (Zevenbergen, Whitehurst, & Zevenbergen, 2003). Both the PEER and CROWD strategies allow the child to become more interactive with the shared book. See Table 1 for definitions and examples.

Mrs. Houze often uses DR in her speech-language therapy, particularly when providing instruction to young children with language impairments. To make sure that she uses all strategies in the CROWD and PEER techniques, she reads a story in advance and writes prompts on sticky notes throughout the book. The advanced reading and prompts also remind her to address all the children's goals. For example, if a child is working on wh-questions, she will make sure to ask him the wh prompts of CROWD. Further, if a child is working toward speaking in complete sentences, Mrs. Houze will be sure to use the "expand" prompt of PEER. Mrs. Houze made notes about her strategies to meet the children's goals to share in her collaboration meeting with Mr. Stanfield.

Mr. Stanfield had limited time for collaborating with other school professionals because state regulations do not allow him to stay after school for more

> When using appreciative inquiry, professionals create change by using positive language and collective inquiry to lead the team to the ideal future.

Table 1
Dialogic Reading Strategies

Domain	Dimension	Definition
Prompt		
Completion	Adult leaves a "blank" at the end of the sentence for the child to fill in	"And the caterpillar was still _____."
Recall	Adult asks question about events or main ideas in the story	"What did the caterpillar eat first?"
Open-Ended	Adult encourages child to describe what is happening in a picture	"Now you tell me what happened on this page."
Wh– Question	Adult asks who, what, when, where, why questions about the story, particularly vocabulary	"Where was the little egg?"
Distancing	Adult asks child to relate events in story to their experiences	"When you get hungry like the caterpillar, what do you eat?"
Evaluate	Adult praises correct or incorrect responses	"Yes, the caterpillar is eating an apple."
Expand	Adult expands the child's response by restating and adding more information	"Yes, the caterpillar is eating a juicy red apple."
Repeat	Adult asks the child to repeat the expansion	"Say that again. What is the caterpillar eating?"

than 30 minutes. Therefore, Mrs. Houze had to be creative in this collaboration and acknowledge that the process would take several months. Mrs. Houze and Mr. Stanfield met to discuss the first phase of AI: definition. The two professionals decided to use dialogic reading to help Mr. Stanfield learn how to better support the children with communication delays. They also decided to meet on Mondays and Wednesdays after school to collaborate. Mrs. Houze started the collaborative teaming by asking Mr. Stanfield to observe her using DR during a storybook reading while providing her in-class speech-language services. Additionally, she observed him reading a storybook. After school, they reported what they observed, describing in positive language (AI phase: discovery) and discussed the ideal classroom collaboration among the teacher, paraprofessional, and related service personnel (AI phase: dream). The next week, Mrs. Houze and Mr. Stanfield designed their plan (AI phase: design). Mrs. Houze provided Mr. Stanfield with materials on DR, particularly the CROWD and PEER strategies. The subsequent time Mrs. Houze was in the classroom, she asked Mr. Stanfield to check off each time she used a strategy so he could see them in action on a DR checklist. This also *allowed Mr. Stanfield to actively participate while observing. Mrs. Houze then showed Mr. Stanfield how she gave herself visual reminders within the books.*

Mrs. Houze wanted to make sure this was a collaborative opportunity, rather than a training, because she felt that if she collaborated with Mr. Stanfield, he would have a greater buy-in to the DR intervention and she would learn much from him as well. Mrs. Houze asked Mr. Stanfield to identify a couple of the children's favorite books. The next week for one afternoon, Mr. Stanfield watched Mrs. Houze create sticky note prompts based on the CROWD and PEER strategies within one of the books. The following day, Mr. Stanfield created his sticky note prompts with Mrs. Houze. Then, Mr. Stanfield created the sticky note prompts independently. Over the next two weeks, Mrs. Houze stayed in the classroom an extra 10 minutes and observed Mr. Stanfield complete storybook readings, providing feedback after school when appropriate. The after-school feedback sessions consisted of conversations regarding the students' progress on their language goals, discussions on the positive aspects of the storybook session, and mutual problem-solving when the readings did not go as planned.

Steps for Establishing an SLP–Paraprofessional Collaboration on Dialogic Reading

Step 1: Collaborate and reflect using strength-based approach. Each team member enters the collaboration with an open mind, where it is understood that all members bring strengths and opportunities to grow in the collaboration. This allows for building team capacity through the exchange of expertise, knowledge, and skills (TC2). The team members may decide to implement the AI approach, in which all members of the collaboration would define their role and goals (AI phase: definition), discuss the positives and strengths of the current system in place when student behaviors and outcomes are optimal (AI phase: discovery), and dream of what this collaboration could create in the future (AI phase: dream). The team members then decide on the principles that guide the changes in their dream model (AI phase: design) and implement the model or the collaboration (AI phase: destiny). This process allows for open communication that enhances the team members' relationship (TC3).

Step 2: SLP observation. The SLP observes the paraprofessional engage in a typical storybook reading with students. The SLP collects notes on the paraprofessional's strengths and opportunities to grow, then provides feedback on those strengths (TC3).

Step 3: Foundational knowledge on dialogic reading. The SLP provides the paraprofessional with foundational knowledge of dialogic reading, such as the purpose of the intervention, the effectiveness of DR, and definitions of CROWD and PEER with examples (TC2; see Table 1). See Buysse, Winton, Rous, Epstein, and Cavanaugh (2011) for an additional resource on DR.

Step 4: Model of a dialogic reading session. The SLP models a DR session with a small group of children in the classroom. During this time, the paraprofessional observes the SLP in a DR session and notes the DR strategies being implemented via a checklist and notes. The paraprofessional provides strength-based feedback to the SLP. See Figure 1 for a sample checklist (TC2).

> Each team member enters the collaboration with an open mind, where it is understood that all members bring strengths and opportunities to grow in the collaboration.

Figure 1
Dialogic Reading Checklist

Components observed		Circle response	
Prompt/Question ☐ Completion ☐ Recall ☐ Open-ended ☐ Wh–? ☐ Distancing ☐ Vocabulary ☐ Other Question or Word: _____		Yes	No
	Evaluates	Yes	No
	Expands	Yes	No
	Repeats	Yes	No
Prompt/Question ☐ Completion ☐ Recall ☐ Open-ended ☐ Wh–? ☐ Distancing ☐ Vocabulary ☐ Other Question or Word: _____		Yes	No
	Evaluates	Yes	No
	Expands	Yes	No
	Repeats	Yes	No
Prompt/Question ☐ Completion ☐ Recall ☐ Open-ended ☐ Wh–? ☐ Distancing ☐ Vocabulary ☐ Other Question or Word: _____		Yes	No
	Evaluates	Yes	No
	Expands	Yes	No
	Repeats	Yes	No
Prompt/Question ☐ Completion ☐ Recall ☐ Open-ended ☐ Wh–? ☐ Distancing ☐ Vocabulary ☐ Other Question or Word: _____		Yes	No
	Evaluates	Yes	No
	Expands	Yes	No
	Repeats	Yes	No

Step 5: Paraprofessional implementation. Prior to the paraprofessional's initial implementation, the SLP and paraprofessional work together to write DR prompts on sticky notes to place throughout the book. The SLP then observes the paraprofessional's story times when possible and provides feedback as needed or desired, using a strength-based AI approach. The SLP will encourage the paraprofessional to write prompts within subsequent books, with assistance from the SLP as needed.

Step 6: Monitoring and fidelity. To maintain both a collaborative approach and ensure DR is implemented with fidelity by the paraprofessional, the SLP observes a portion of the reading session implemented by the paraprofessional during her weekly visits to the preschool classroom. The SLP can use a checklist to monitor which DR strategies the paraprofessional uses and which may need to be reinforced through modeling or feedback (see Figure 2 for a sample

Figure 2
Dialogic Reading Monitoring and Fidelity Checklist

Complete the chart below with total numbers across book reading.

Feature	Total number
Completion prompts	
Recall questions	
Open-ended questions	
Wh– questions	
Distancing questions	
Vocabulary questions	

Complete the chart below with total number across each book reading.

Feature	Total number observed	Total number possible	Percentage
Pause 3–5 seconds			
Repeat prompt			
Evaluates			
Expands			
Asks child to repeat			

checklist). As the school year progresses, these check-ins will become less frequent unless a decrease in the use of the DR strategies is noted (TC1, TC2).

Conclusion

Collaborative practices in educational settings, particularly those between paraprofessionals and related service personnel such as SLPs, are one approach to improve outcomes for preschool children with disabilities. The AI framework provides a strength-based approach for professionals to collaborate in a safe and positive manner. Using AI, paraprofessionals can provide supplementary services to children that focus on academic needs, allowing the children more opportunities to practice targeted language skills. While this article features collaborations between just two types of professionals, this approach shows utility for many different collaborative teams and families.

References

Allen, S. J., & Graden, J. L. (2002). Best practices in collaborative problem solving for intervention design. In A. Thomas & J. Grimes (Eds.), *Best practices in school psychology* (4th ed., pp. 565–582). Bethesda, MD: National Association of School Psychologists.

American Speech-Language-Hearing Association. (2010). Roles and responsibilities of speech-language pathologists in schools [Position statement]. Retrieved from https://www.asha.org/policy/ps2010-00318/

American Speech-Language-Hearing Association. (2014). *Schools survey report: SLP caseload characteristics trends 1995–2014.* Rockville, MD: Author.

Aram, D. M., Ekelman, B. L., & Nation, J. E. (1984). Preschoolers with language disorders: 10 years later. *Journal of Speech, Language, and Hearing Research, 27,* 232–244. doi:10.1044/jshr.2702.244

Bucholz, J. L., & Green, K. B. (2018). Characteristics of individuals with disabilities. In J. L. Bucholz & S. H. Robbins (Eds.), *Special education: An introduction for all educators* (pp. 62–87). Dubuque, IA: Kendall Hunt.

Buysse, V., Winton, P., Rous, B., Epstein, D., & Cavanaugh, C. (2011). CONNECT Module 6: Dialogic reading practices [Web-based professional development curriculum]. Chapel Hill: University of North Carolina, FPG Child Development Institute. Retrieved from http://community.fpg.unc.edu/connect-modules/learners/module-6

Calabrese, R., Hester, M., Friesen, S., & Burkhalter, K. (2010). Using appreciative inquiry to create a sustainable rural school district and community. *International Journal of Educational Management, 24,* 250–265. doi:10.1108/09513541011031592

Carlson, E., Bitterman, A., & Jenkins, F. (2012). Home literacy environment and its role in the achievement of preschoolers with disabilities. *The Journal of Special Education, 46,* 67–77. doi:10.1177/0022466910371229

Causton-Theoharis, J. N., & Malmgren, K. W. (2005). Increasing peer interactions for students with severe disabilities via paraprofessional training. *Exceptional Children, 71,* 431–444. doi:10.1177/001440290507100403

Chopra, R. V., Sandoval-Lucero, E., Aragon, L., Bernal, C., De Balderas, H. B., & Carroll, D. (2004). The paraprofessional role of connector. *Remedial and Special Education, 25,* 219–231. doi:10.1177/07419325040250040501

Cobb, C. (2007). Training paraprofessionals to effectively work with all students. *The Reading Teacher, 60,* 686–689. doi:10.1598/RT.60.7.10

Cooperrider, D. L., & Whitney, D. (2005). *Appreciative inquiry: A positive revolution in change.* San Francisco, CA: Berrett-Koehler.

Cooperrider, D. L., Whitney, D., & Stavros, J. M. (2008). *Appreciative inquiry handbook: For leaders of change* (2nd ed.). San Francisco, CA: Berrett-Koehler.

Dickerson, M. S., & Helm-Stevens, R. (2011). Reculturing schools for greater impact: Using appreciative inquiry as a non-coercive change process. *International Journal of Business and Management, 6*(8), 66–74. doi:10.5539/ijbm.v6n8p66

Division for Early Childhood. (2014). *DEC recommended practices in early intervention/early childhood special education 2014*. Retrieved from http://www.dec-sped.org/dec-recommended-practices

Filleul, M., & Rowland, B. (2006, June). Using appreciative inquiry in the Vancouver School District: A positive approach to enhance learning. *BC Educational Leadership Research*, 1–10. Retrieved from http://www.aceconsulting.ca/ai/Using_Appreciative_Inquiry.pdf

Fleury, V. P., Miramontez, S. H., Hudson, R. F., & Schwartz, I. S. (2014). Promoting active participation in book reading for preschoolers with Autism Spectrum Disorder: A preliminary study. *Child Language Teaching and Therapy, 30*, 273–288. doi:10.1177/0265659013514069

French, N. K. (2003). Paraeducators in special education programs. *Focus on Exceptional Children, 36*, 1–16.

Goddard, Y. L., Goddard, R. D., & Tschannen-Moran, M. (2007). A theoretical and empirical investigation of teacher collaboration for school improvement and student achievement in public elementary schools. *Teachers College Record, 109*, 877–896.

Hall, L. J., Grundon, G. S., Pope, C., & Romero, A. B. (2010). Training paraprofessionals to use behavioral strategies when educating learners with autism spectrum disorders across environments. *Behavioral Interventions, 25*, 37–51. doi:10.1002/bin.294

Hus, Y. (2014). Educators specializing in language stimulation: Extending speech-language pathology services via paraprofessional training. *Speech and Hearing Review: A Bilingual Annual, 12*, 103–124.

Idol, L., Nevin, A., & Paolucci-Whitcomb, P. (2000). *Collaborative consultation* (3rd ed.). Austin, TX: PRO-ED.

Killoran, J., Templeman, T. P., Peters, J., & Udell, T. (2001). Identifying paraprofessional competencies for early intervention and early childhood special education. *Teaching Exceptional Children, 34*, 68–73. doi:10.1177/004005990103400109

Koppenhaver, D. A., Hendrix, M. P., & Williams, A. R. (2007, February). Toward evidence-based literacy interventions for children with severe and multiple disabilities. *Seminars in Speech and Language, 28*, 79–89. doi:10.1055/s-2007-967932

Ledford, J. R., Zimmerman, K. N., Chazin, K. T., Patel, N. M., Morales, V. A., & Bennett, B. P. (2017). Coaching paraprofessionals to promote engagement and social interactions during small group activities. *Journal of Behavioral Education, 26*, 410–432. doi:10.1007/s10864-017-9273-8

Ledford, J. R., Zimmerman, K. N., Harbin, E. R., & Ward, S. E. (2017). Improving the use of evidence-based instructional practices for paraprofessionals. *Focus on Autism and Other Developmental Disabilities.* Advance online publication. doi:10.1177/1088357617699178

Lonigan, C. J., & Whitehurst, G. J. (1998). Relative efficacy of parent and teacher involvement in a shared-reading intervention for preschool children from low-income backgrounds. *Early Childhood Research Quarterly, 13*, 263–290. doi:10.1016/S0885-2006(99)80038-6

Marvin, C. (1994). Home literacy experiences of preschool children with single and multiple disabilities. *Topics in Early Childhood Special Education, 14,* 436–454. doi:10.1177/027112149401400405

National Institute of Child Health and Human Development Early Child Care Research Network. (2005). Pathways to reading: The role of oral language in the transition to reading. *Developmental Psychology, 41,* 428–442. doi:10.1037/0012-1649.41.2.428

Odom, S. L., & Wolery, M. (2003). A unified theory of practice in early intervention/early childhood special education: Evidence-based practices. *The Journal of Special Education, 37,* 164–173. doi:10.1177/00224669030370030601

Pugach, M. C., Blanton, L. P., Correa, V. I., McLeskey, J., & Langley, L. K. (2009, September). *The role of collaboration in supporting the induction and retention of new special education teachers* (NCIPP Document No. RS-2ES). Gainesville, FL: National Center to Inform Policy and Practice in Special Education Professional Development.

Riggs, C. G. (2001). Ask the paraprofessionals: What are your training needs? *Teaching Exceptional Children, 33,* 78–83. doi:10.1177/004005990103300312

Schooling, T. L. (2003, August). Lessons from the National Outcomes Measurement System (NOMS). *Seminars in Speech and Language, 24,* 245–256. doi:10.1055/s-2003-42827

Schrage, M. (1995). *No more teams! Mastering the dynamics of creative collaboration.* New York, NY: Currency Doubleday.

Towson, J. A., Gallagher, P. A., & Bingham, G. E. (2016). Dialogic reading: Language and preliteracy outcomes for young children with disabilities. *Journal of Early Intervention, 38,* 230–246. doi:10.1177/1053815116668643

Trautman, M. L. (2004). Preparing and managing paraprofessionals. *Intervention in School and Clinic, 39,* 131–138. doi:10.1177/10534512040390030101

U.S. Department of Education. (2004, March). *Title 1 paraprofessionals non-regulatory guide.* Retrieved from https://www2.ed.gov/policy/elsec/guid/paraguidance.pdf

Vasa, S., Steckelberg, A., & Pickett, A. L. (2003). Paraeducators in educational settings: Administrative issues. In A. L. Pickett & K. Gerlach (Eds.), *Supervising paraeducators in educational settings: A team approach* (2nd ed., pp. 255–288). Austin, TX: PRO-ED.

Wallace, T. (2004). Paraprofessionals in schools: Topics for administrators. *Journal of Special Education Leadership, 17,* 46–61.

Waters, L., & White, M. (2015). Case study of a school wellbeing initiative: Using appreciative inquiry to support positive change. *International Journal of Wellbeing, 5,* 19–32. doi:10.5502/ijw.v5i1.2

Watkins, J. M., Mohr, B. J., & Kelly, R. (2011). *Appreciative inquiry: Change at the speed of imagination* (2nd ed). San Francisco, CA: Pfeiffer.

Wermer, L., Brock, M. E., & Seaman, R. L. (2017). Efficacy of a teacher training a paraprofessional to promote communication for a student with autism and complex communication needs. *Focus on Autism and Other Developmental Disabilities.* Advance online publication. doi:10.1177/1088357617736052

What Works Clearinghouse. (2007, February). Dialogic reading (WWC intervention report). Washington, DC: U.S. Department of Educational Institute of Education Sciences.

Zevenbergen, A. A., Whitehurst, G. J., & Zevenbergen, J. A. (2003). Effects of a shared-reading intervention on the inclusion of evaluative devices in narratives of children from low-income families. *Journal of Applied Developmental Psychology, 24,* 1–15. doi:10.1016/S0193-3973(03)00021-2

4

Developing a Collaborative Partnership to Enhance Teaming
Using a Practice-Based Coaching Framework

Darbianne Shannon
Crystal Bishop
Patricia Snyder
Jennifer Jaramillo
University of Florida

Michael has worked in the local Head Start program for just more than a year as the lead teacher alongside his teaching assistant, Myrna, who has worked in the program for 12 years. They both love teaching and feel they are making a difference in the lives of children from their community. They are proud of their knowledge of the Head Start Early Learning Outcomes Framework (ELOF; Office of Head Start, 2015) and are committed to providing an environment that helps children learn and prepares them for kindergarten. Michael and Myrna collaborate each week to plan for and provide a variety of opportunities for children to communicate with adults and peers, make choices, acquire social skills through interactions with their peers, and develop preacademic skills using developmentally appropriate materials.

This year, Michael and Myrna's classroom of sixteen 3- and 4-year-olds includes a child named Tavion, who recently began receiving early childhood special education services. Tavion joined the classroom in October, shortly after his third birthday. The goals on his individualized education program (IEP) are focused on social-emotional and language skills. His speech-language therapist, Karen, comes from a local agency three times per week for 20 minutes each visit. She brings materials and provides one-on-one services in the classroom. Michael also tries to work on Tavion's IEP goals during small group rotations in the afternoon.

Michael and Myrna wanted to give Tavion time to adjust to the classroom, but now it is nearly the end of December and Tavion is still communicating mostly through gestures and about 10 single words. In addition, he spends all of center time engaged in solitary play. Michael has never worked with children with disabilities before, and he feels as though his bag of "teaching tools" has been exhausted. Feeling a bit defeated, Michael e-mailed Yesenia, the Head Start disability coordinator, and asked for help. Yesenia and Michael talked about how the team could use embedded instruction to provide more opportunities throughout the day for Tavion to work on targeted skills that are aligned with his IEP goals, the preschool curriculum, and the ELOF. Yesenia explained to Michael that embedded instruction is an intentional and systematic approach for promoting children's acquisition, maintenance, and generalization of skills that support a child's access to and participation in the general preschool curriculum (Snyder, Hemmeter, McLean, Sandall, & McLaughlin, 2013; Snyder et al., 2018). Michael wants to try embedded instruction, but he is concerned about how the team will learn to use it effectively, given all the other demands on their time. In response to his concerns, Yesenia offers to coach the team using a collaborative approach called practice-based coaching. Michael is not sure exactly what this will involve or how he feels about having someone in his classroom to "coach" him and his team, but he decides to schedule a meeting with Yesenia so he and Myrna can learn more.

Practice-based coaching provides the follow-up implementation support for practitioners to transfer what they have learned from other professional development experiences to their classrooms.

Using Practice-based Coaching to Enhance Teacher's Competence and Confidence

In this article, we discuss how structural and process components of practice-based coaching (PBC; Snyder, Hemmeter, & Fox, 2015) can support the development of a collaborative partnership and sustainable communication strategies to enhance the ability of a team (i.e., Michael, Myrna, and Karen) to acquire and become more competent and confident in their use of evidence-based teaching practices to support a young child with a disability in an inclusive preschool classroom. In the example provided, the practice focus of PBC is embedded instruction. Three Division for Early Childhood (DEC) Recommended Practices (2014) related to teaming and collaboration (TC1, TC2, and TC3) are addressed. PBC is a collaborative form of coaching that, when used as intended across a variety of delivery formats, has been shown to be efficacious for supporting preschool teachers to use evidence-based teaching practices and, in turn, improving child outcomes (Snyder, Hemmeter, & Fox, 2015). PBC is a cyclical coaching framework composed of three components: (1) shared goal setting and action planning, including a strengths and needs assessment; (2) focused observation; and (3) reflection and feedback (see Figure 1). These components occur within the context of a collaborative coaching partnership and can be implemented with teachers, related service professionals, family members, or teams to promote collaboration and teaming to implement evidence-based practices that support the development and learning of young children.[1] Throughout this article, we refer to the "coachee" within the PBC partnership as the teaching team, which includes Michael (lead teacher), Myrna (teaching assistant), and Karen (speech language therapist).

PBC typically occurs in conjunction with other professional development experiences where practitioners are acquiring or enhancing knowledge and skills related to a set of evidence-based practices. Use of PBC provides the follow-up implementation support for practitioners to transfer what they have learned

Figure 1
Key Components of the Practice-Based Coaching Framework

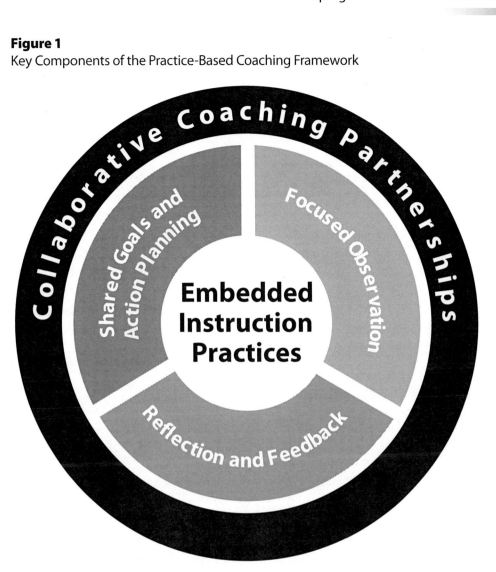

From "Supporting Implementation of Evidence-Based Practices Through Practice-Based Coaching," by P. A. Snyder, M. L. Hemmeter, and L. Fox, 2015, *Topics in Early Childhood Special Education, 35*, p. 135.

from other professional development experiences to their classrooms. In this article, we describe how PBC is implemented when the coach provides on-site support to the coachee. The process of completing a strengths and needs assessment allows the coachee and the coach to identify and discuss the coachee's strengths with respect to the practices that are the focus of coaching as well as priorities for coaching support. When both the coachee and the coach have completed the strengths and needs assessment, they are able to collaborate to identify a shared goal and action plan for implementing a specific teaching practice over the course of two to five weeks. Once a shared goal has been established and the action plan developed, the coach conducts focused observations of the coachee implementing practices and action steps that are the focus of the action plan in the classroom. During the focused observation, the coach collects qualitative and quantitative data about the coachee's use of targeted teaching practices and children's responses to those practices. Data from the focused observation are shared during a debrief meeting, which involves dedicated time for collaborative reflection and the provision of supportive and constructive feedback to enhance the coachee's use of the practice(s) that are the focus of the goal and action plan. These components of the PBC framework are repeated across multiple coaching sessions, each of which includes a focused observation followed by a debrief meeting.

To ensure PBC is used as intended within the context of a collaborative partnership, it is helpful to consider three underlying dimensions of coaching: content, structure, and process (Powell & Diamond, 2013; Snyder, Hemmeter, & McLaughlin, 2011). Content specifies the evidence-based teaching practices that are the focus of coaching (e.g., embedded instruction practices). Structure defines how and how often coaching interactions occur and includes materials to guide how the key components of the PBC framework are used (i.e., coaching manuals, documents to support collaborative interactions). Process includes strategies used by the coach to facilitate interactions between the coach and the coachee(s) and among all members of the child's instructional team.

Establishing the Parameters of the Collaborative Partnership

Yesenia, Michael, Myrna, and Karen represent different disciplines and are guided by diverse philosophies for supporting children and families. To work collaboratively, they will need to use effective communication strategies to develop mutual agreements about their roles and responsibilities within their collaborative partnership and to establish transparency about what interactional strategies will be used both as part of coaching and as they implement embedded instruction to support Tavion (TC2, TC3). Within the PBC framework, coaches use two documents to facilitate effective communication related to the roles, responsibilities, and interactional strategies of team members within the collaborative partnership: a coaching agreement and a preferred coaching strategies checklist.

A coaching agreement describes the actions and behaviors the coach and team agree to do within the collaborative partnership. Typically, this document includes four to six agreements each for the coach and for the team. For example, as the coach, Yesenia agreed to "communicate with the team prior to modeling or interacting with children in the classroom during the observation." This agreement is important for Michael and Myrna, who are feeling hesitant about incorporating another adult into their established classroom activities and routines. An example of a coachee agreement is, "Our team will set aside 30 minutes of uninterrupted time to debrief with our coach every other week." This agreement helps to ensure the team is dedicating a sufficient amount of time to the coaching process and to learning how to use embedded instruction teaching practices as intended. Stating agreements for how to be a collaborative partner allows the coach and team to be transparent about what they will contribute to ensure the productivity of the collaborative partnership.

A preferred coaching strategies checklist describes the essential coaching strategies that are required as part of implementing PBC as intended. It also includes a menu of enhancement strategies that might be used, depending on the

> Stating agreements for how to be a collaborative partner allows the coach and team to be transparent about what they will contribute to ensure the productivity of the collaborative partnership.

individual learning preferences and needs of each member of the teaching team. Within the PBC framework, there are five essential strategies used in all coaching sessions: (1) observation by the coach of the team implementing practices that are the focus of coaching; (2) reflective conversation (i.e., discussion between the coach and the team designed to prompt thinking about implementation of teaching practices that are the focus of coaching); (3) supportive performance feedback (i.e., explicit and descriptive feedback about what the team is doing well in relationship to the evidence-based teaching practices and action plan goal or steps); (4) constructive performance feedback (i.e., objective description of the team's actions or behaviors in the classroom followed by two to three strategies for how the team might enhance its use of the evidence-based teaching practices); and (5) the provision of resources to support the team's implementation of practices that are the focus of coaching.

Video models, problem-solving discussions, gestural prompting, or role play are enhancement coaching strategies that might be used to support the use of a

practice, but they might not be necessary in every coaching session. While most strategies can be used during both the focused observation in the classroom and the debrief meeting (e.g., supportive performance feedback, modeling), some are most appropriate for the focused observation (e.g., gestural prompting) or the debrief meeting (e.g., video models). In the initial coaching session, the team can ask questions about each of the coaching strategies and indicate which enhancement strategies they want the coach to use when supporting its use of targeted teaching practices. The coaching strategies checklist can be reviewed at multiple points throughout the coaching cycle because preferences for enhancement strategies might evolve as the partnership develops with the coach and among team members.

Structural documents such as a coaching agreement and a preferred coaching strategies checklist can help coaches and teams to enhance communication and promote individualization and choice. They help set the foundation for a transactional collaborative partnership and effective teaming in the classroom. Use of structures to document these choices can also help teachers and related service professionals communicate with each other by serving as a reminder of their mutual agreement to participate collaboratively in the coaching process and as a member of the team. These documents might also help the team identify enhancement strategies they can use to support each other between coaching sessions. For example, Michael, Myrna, and Karen might decide that Michael or Myrna will videotape Tavion during ongoing classroom activities so all three team members can review the video clips to discuss how Tavion is progressing toward his learning objectives and so Karen can provide some suggestions for strategies they can use to facilitate Tavion's communication.

Yesenia uses a coaching agreement to describe further the commitments the team would need to make to engage in PBC and the preferred coaching strategies checklist to explain ways she might interact with the team and the children during the focused observation in the classroom and the debrief meeting. Michael asks questions about how she will use performance feedback, and Myrna asks about what she will be looking for during the observation. Yesenia also describes the enhancement strategies and encourages Michael and Myrna to share the preferred coaching strategies checklist with Karen so they can discuss as a team how they would like Yesenia to be involved in the classroom during the focused observation, how they might support one another between coaching sessions, and how Yesenia could provide support in the debrief.

Although somewhat apprehensive going into the meeting, Michael and Myrna

leave feeling much more comfortable with PBC. They appreciate that Yesenia acknowledged their strengths and are relieved she is not going to use coaching strategies that are uncomfortable for the team. Michael and Myrna schedule time to review the preferred coaching strategies checklist with Karen when she visits the program on Wednesday. The team decides they are not comfortable reviewing video of themselves at this early stage in coaching, but they would like to see video exemplars of other teachers using embedded instruction. They also would like Yesenia to model using embedded instruction practices during focused observations and to use role play in the debrief to help them plan for and practice using embedded instruction teaching practices. To get started, Yesenia sends the team a link to view an online module that includes a description and video exemplars of embedded instruction practices.

Using the Strengths and Needs Assessment to Set a Goal and Develop an Action Plan

As the team moves into its initial coaching sessions, they begin to focus more on the evidence-based teaching practices at the core of the PBC framework. Two documents are used to guide the coach and team through a systematic conversation about which teaching practices are priorities for their classroom: a strengths and needs assessment and an action plan.

A strengths and needs assessment lists the teaching practices that are the focus of coaching and provides a way for the coach and team to each record information about (a) what practices the team is using in the classroom, (b) how often and with what level of competence and confidence the team is using each practice, and (c) whether the team would like support to enhance their use of each teaching practice. The strengths and needs assessment documents completed by the coach and team are then used for collaborative goal setting and action planning. Generally, goal setting and action planning begins by providing teams with an opportunity to discuss their strengths and needs assessment ratings, while the coach highlights similarities and differences between the team's ratings and the coach's ratings. As the strengths and needs assessment ratings are discussed, the coach and team collaborate to develop an observable and measurable teaching goal, which states the teaching practice that will be the focus of the coaching interactions for two to five weeks. The teaching goal is recorded on an action plan document followed by a criterion to know when the goal has been met, action steps outlining coach and team member actions for achieving the goal, resources, and a timeline.

An action plan document is an essential structural feature of the PBC process because it guides (a) what teams will do to enhance their use of evidence-based teaching practices on a daily or weekly basis, (b) what the coach will look for and how the coach will collect data during the focused observation, and (c) what the focus of the reflective conversation, performance-based feedback, and shared resources and materials will be in the debrief meeting. An action plan is also used systematically at each coaching debrief meeting to help the team reflect on progress toward achieving its teaching goal and, when necessary, to negotiate changes to the agreed-upon roles and process for achieving the goal. Goal setting and action planning, including a strengths and needs assessment, provide a process for teams to work together to identify how they will exchange expertise, knowledge, and information to build their capacity to plan, implement, and evaluate practices that will promote optimal child outcomes. Collaborative decisions and plans for implementing and evaluating their use of practices that are the focus of coaching are documented on the action plan so all team members have a shared language and structure to guide their practice as they work to achieve their shared goal.

> **"**
>
> Goal setting and action planning, including a strengths and needs assessment, provide a process for teams to work together to identify how they will exchange expertise, knowledge, and information.

Michael, Myrna, and Karen complete an online embedded instruction module together after school and discuss what practices they are familiar with and what practices they feel they need the most support from Yesenia to use. On Wednesday, during snack and center time, Yesenia visits the classroom for about an hour to observe the teaching team's ongoing interactions in the classroom with all children and Tavion. She sits off to the side of the room and records notes on the strengths and needs assessment document about the team's current use of six embedded-instruction teaching practices and areas where she believes she could provide support to enhance their instruction for all children and Tavion.

During nap time, the team meets to debrief. Yesenia begins by giving the team a blank copy of the strengths and needs assessment document and asking them to reflect together and share their thoughts about their strengths and needs with respect to the embedded instruction teaching practices. Yesenia also shares notes from her focused observation and strengths and needs assessment, highlighting

Figure 2
Michael, Myrna, and Karen's Action Plan

Teaching goal

We will write two priority learning targets (PLTs) for Tavion and will practice embedding learning opportunities on these targets in two or more classroom activities and routines.

Criterion

We will know we have achieved this goal when we are providing opportunities for Tavion to work on each of his two PLTs during two or more activities per day for one week.

	Steps to achieve this goal	Resources needed	Timeline
1	Michael, Myrna, and Karen will review examples of observable and measurable PLTs.	Website, sample PLTs	12/3
2	Michael and Myrna will video Tavion interacting in ongoing activities, routines, and transitions and share the video with Karen.	Video camera, memory card to store video and give to Karen	12/4
3	Michael, Myrna, and Karen review Tavion's current IEP goals and video clips to determine appropriate target skills and write two observable and measurable PLTs that are proximal to Tavion's current skill level.	Tavion's IEP goals, video clips of Tavion, team planning time	12/6
4	Michael e-mails PLTs to Yesenia to receive feedback and includes Myrna and Karen on e-mails.	E-mail, coach time	12/6
5	Michael and Myrna implement learning opportunities for two PLTs during one activity or routine while Yesenia collects data.	Team planning time, coach time	12/9
6	Michael, Myrna, and Yesenia discuss and identify a second logical activity or routine in which to embed learning opportunities for each PLT.	Coach and team planning time, planning forms	12/9
7	With Karen's support, Michael and Myrna provide opportunities for Tavion to practice each PLT skill during two or more planned activities and they collect data about their implementation and Tavion's demonstration of the targeted skills.	Planning forms, data collection system, team planning time	12/15

many things the team is doing well. As they discuss their strengths and needs assessment ratings, Michael, Myrna, Karen, and Yesenia agree their teaching goal and action plan (see Figure 2) will focus on writing two priority learning targets (PLTs) for Tavion based on his IEP goals and embedding learning opportunities for each PLT.

To start on their first action step, Yesenia reminds the team that PLTs should be proximal behaviors or skills just beyond Tavion's current level. Karen shares some of the data she has collected about Tavion's current ability to communicate based on the IEP goals and explains how important it is that the team consistently require Tavion to use his words, even if they know what he wants based on his gestures. Yesenia thanks Karen for her expertise, and they all agree Tavion needs support to make verbal requests. Yesenia shows examples of high-quality PLTs and describes how the team might try to provide embedded learning opportunities for Tavion to make one- to two-word requests for objects at meal times. They role play how opportunities might be provided in these activities as they wrap up the coaching session. Yesenia then asks whether there is anything specific they would like for her to observe and provide feedback on during her next visit. The team asks her to count how many opportunities they provide for Tavion to make one- to two-word requests during meals and to help them think about other natural opportunities for him to practice this skill. As they leave the meeting, Michael says, "I like the idea of helping Tavion work on his IEP goals without developing special activities just for him. I knew it didn't feel right to work with him separately on his IEP goals, but I just didn't know what else to try."

Reflection and Performance Feedback Guided by the Coaching Protocol

In each PBC session, the coach conducts a focused observation guided by the action plan and then engages with the team in a debrief meeting of approximately 30 minutes. The debrief meeting is guided by a coaching log (Snyder, Hemmeter, Bishop, Shannon, & McLean, 2015) that includes 10–15 actions or behaviors the coach will use to facilitate reflection and discussion among team members about their use of the evidence-based teaching practices in the classroom. Coaching log items address key components of the PBC framework and help the coach and team members (a) reflect on the current action plan and what occurred during the observation, (b) use qualitative and quantitative data collected during the focused observation to provide each other with supportive and constructive performance feedback that moves the team toward achieving the action plan goal, and (c) discuss what resources or materials are needed to address the constructive feedback and next action step. A coaching log is a structural support that reminds the coach of the logical sequence for the debrief discussion and the essential strategies the coach and team members will engage in to continue to develop their collaborative partnership and to achieve the positive results associated with prior studies employing the PBC framework (Snyder, Hemmeter, & Fox, 2015; Snyder et al., 2018). A coaching log also provides a routine structure that lets team members know what to expect during the debrief meeting, increasing the likelihood they will be prepared and feel confident contributing their thoughts and ideas as they collaboratively work toward the action plan goal (Shannon, Snyder, & McLaughlin, 2015).

Before the second coaching session, Yesenia gathers resources that could help the team consider when it might provide additional learning opportunities for Tavion to work on his language PLTs. She also brings instructional plans that might help the team plan for how it will provide learning opportunities for Tavion's PLT by using materials in a variety of activities and routines. During the focused observation, Yesenia uses tallies to document the number of opportunities the team provides for Tavion to make one- to two-word requests at meals. She also makes notes about natural opportunities she observes during centers.

During the coaching debrief meeting, Yesenia positions the action plan and data she collected so it will be available for her and the team to reference. Yesenia thanks the team for the opportunity to visit and facilitates data-based team reflection.

She says, "I noticed Tavion said 'crackers' and pointed to the box two times during the first 10 minutes of snack today! What do you think was different about snack time today that encouraged him to use words?" Michael and Myrna shared that Karen had suggested that they place the cracker box in sight, but out of reach, to encourage Tavion to verbally request crackers. She modeled this environmental arrangement strategy for them last week.

Yesenia provided supportive feedback by stating, "It is terrific that you are working together as a team to think about how you can provide embedded learning opportunities for Tavion during meals and that you're using your team members to model!" Myrna said, "Michael and I have also been reminding each other to provide a consequence when Tavion makes a one- to two-word request. Like today, Michael got interrupted when Lilybeth spilled her milk. So, I said, 'Tavion, I like the way you used your words to ask for crackers!'" A warm smile spread across Yesenia's face as she said, "Providing consequences immediately after Tavion makes a one- to two-word request is going to ensure he continues to use his words. It's great that you're able to remind each other about these embedded instruction practices!"

Yesenia glances at her coaching log, action plan, and her notes about how the team might enhance their instruction and says, "I noticed snack was the only time during the day that Tavion used his words to request objects. For him to increase his language, he will need more opportunities to practice. One way you might increase the number of opportunities for Tavion to practice making one- to two-word requests would be to develop an activity matrix for the team to collaboratively plan for times of day that are a natural or logical fit for the PLTs."

Yesenia shared photos of activity matrices, explained the parts of the matrices, and described how they could be used. "Another option would be to develop an instructional plan that you might use to guide your interactions during particular activities or with specific materials Tavion uses often in class. For example, today when another child got Tavion's preferred toy at the train table, he began to cry. Michael, you asked the peer to give the toy to Tavion. Do you think that could have been a good opportunity to help Tavion use one to two words to request the toy? We have discussed two options for how you might increase the number of opportunities provided to Tavion beyond meals. What would be most helpful: the activity matrix, the instructional plan, or something else I didn't think of?" Michael, Myrna, and Karen discussed the benefits and challenges of each option, then they decided to develop an activity matrix so everyone on the team will have a visual reminder of what Tavion is working on during each activity. Yesenia worked with the team to tweak this action step on the team's action plan and said, "I'll e-mail a copy of the updated action plan to you all this afternoon."

Using Structural Features of the PBC Framework to Enhance the Coaching Process

For teams to use teaching practices such as embedded instruction as intended to promote optimal child development and learning (TC1, TC2), they often benefit from the support of coaches to enhance their knowledge and skills and to assist the team in learning how to communicate effectively (TC3) about how each member of the teaching team can contribute to a common instructional goal such as the one Michael, Myrna, and, Karen wrote on their action plan. Through their facilitated debrief meetings with Yesenia, Michael and Myrna began to see Karen as a more accessible resource for identifying skills that would help Tavion achieve his communication goals throughout the day. Karen began to interact more with Michael, Myrna, and Tavion's peers in the classroom. All team members also became more conscious of their use of the embedded instruction practices and provided each other with performance feedback throughout the day and modeled for each other how to effectively provide learning opportunities for Tavion in new activities and routines.

As the team began to feel more confident in its use of embedded instruction and saw that Tavion was making more one- to two-word verbal requests for items in the classroom, they shared information about embedded instruction with Tavion's family. They collected video examples of strategies his family might use to provide opportunities for him to make verbal requests at home. After viewing the video clips, Tavion's family requested a meeting to talk more about how they could use the strategies at home.

Michael, Myrna, and Karen met with Tavion's family and helped them think through their daily activities and routines in their home and community, prioritizing times that would be feasible for them to help Tavion practice making one- to two-word verbal requests. They also wrote a plan for how they could arrange materials in their home environment to promote verbal requests. After three weeks of trying the strategies they discussed, Tavion's family reported he

> For teams to use teaching practices such as embedded instruction as intended to promote optimal child development and learning, they often benefit from the support of coaches to enhance their knowledge and skills and to assist the team in learning how to communicate effectively.

Table 1
Structural PBC Coaching Documents That Facilitate Collaboration and Teaming

Structural documents	Collaborative process (recommended practice)	Key components
Coaching contract	Used to facilitate communication between coach and team members about their roles and responsibilities within the collaborative partnership (TC3).	• 4-6 statements describing actions or behaviors the coach and coachees agree to as part of the collaborative coaching partnership
Preferred coaching strategy checklist	Used to facilitate discussion about the essential coaching strategies the coach will use in all sessions and the enhancement strategies. The coachees can select enhancement strategies to support the implementation of evidence-based practices that will promote optimal child development and learning, based on their individual preferences and needs (TC2, TC3).	• Descriptions and examples of essential coaching strategies (i.e., observation, reflective conversation, supportive performance feedback, constructive performance feedback, and providing resources) • Descriptions and examples of enhancement coaching strategies (e.g., role-play, modeling) • Space for the coachees to indicate which enhancement strategies are preferred
Strengths and needs assessment	Used to facilitate coach's and coachees' reflection and discussion about when and how the coachees are using the evidence-based teaching practices that are the focus of coaching. It also includes information about which teaching practices are a priority for the coachees. This discussion informs the development of shared action plan goals (TC3).	• List of evidence-based teaching practices that are the focus of coaching • System for the coachees and coach to document how the coachees are using the practice (e.g., rating scale) • System for the coachees and coach to document what practices are the highest priorities for coaching (e.g., rating scale, rank-order, open-ended question)

was using words to request at home more frequently and that everyone was feeling less frustrated because Tavion could say what he wanted or needed.

The vignette of Michael, Myrna, Karen, and their coach, Yesenia, illustrates how five documents (see Table 1), which guide the underlying structural features of the PBC framework, can enhance a coach's ability to foster collaborative partnerships among members of a teaching team. The partnership is characterized by clear expectations, a common goal focused on a teaching practice, and responsiveness to individual needs, preferences, and motivations of each team member. Collaboration and communication among the members of the teaching team, along with repeated opportunities for reflection and feedback guided by a coach, can help to ensure evidence-based teaching practices that are the focus of coaching are adopted and sustained as intended in the classroom and at home, supporting optimal outcomes for young children.

Table 1 (continued)
Structural PBC Coaching Documents That Facilitate Collaboration and Teaming

Structural documents	Collaborative process (recommended practice)	Key components
Action plan	Used to record the intended outcome of engaging in PBC and to guide the focused observation and debrief meeting. This document includes a collaboratively developed teaching goal statement about the coachees' enhanced use of an evidence-based teaching practice, a criterion to know when the goal has been met, action steps the coach and coachees will engage in to achieve the goal, resources/materials that will aide the coachees in achieving the goal, and a timeline for goal achievement (TC1, TC2, TC3).	• Goal statement • Criterion statement • Action steps describing what each member of the collaborative partnership will do to achieve the goal • A list of resources (i.e., materials, time, personnel, information) needed to complete each action step • Timelines for completing each action step
Coaching log	Used by the coach to ensure the key components of the PBC framework are implemented as intended in each coaching session (TC2).	• Key actions or behaviors the coach must do to ensure all components of the PBC framework are implemented with fidelity, with space to indicate whether each action or behavior occurred • A list of essential and enhancement strategies, with space to indicate whether each strategy was used in the observation or debrief meeting

Note

1. To date, the use of PBC in collaborative teaming and group delivery formats has not been evaluated through rigorous experimental trials. However, program evaluations conducted in California and New Zealand have shown promise for this delivery format.

References

Division for Early Childhood. (2014). *DEC recommended practices for early intervention/early childhood special education 2014*. Retrieved from http://www.dec-sped.org/dec-recommended-practices

Office of Head Start. (2015). *Head Start early learning outcomes framework: Ages birth to five*. Washington, DC: Author. Retrieved from https://eclkc.ohs.acf.hhs.gov/sites/default/files/pdf/elof-ohs-framework.pdf

Powell, D. R., & Diamond, K. E. (2013). Studying the implementation of coaching-based professional development. In T. Halle, A. Metz, & I. Martinez-Beck (Eds.), *Applying implementation science in early childhood programs and systems* (pp. 97–116). Baltimore, MD: Paul H. Brookes.

Shannon, D., Snyder, P., & McLaughlin, T. (2015). Preschool teachers' insights about web-based self-coaching versus on-site expert coaching. *Professional Development in Education, 41*, 290–309. doi:10.1080/19415257.2014.986819

Snyder, P. A., Hemmeter, M. L., Bishop, C., Shannon, D., & McLean, M. (2015). *Embedded instruction for early learning coach manual* [Protocol and forms]. Unpublished manual. Gainesville: Anita Zucker Center for Excellence in Early Childhood Studies, University of Florida.

Snyder, P. A., Hemmeter, M. L., & Fox, L. (2015). Supporting implementation of evidence-based practices through practice-based coaching. *Topics in Early Childhood Special Education, 35*, 133–143. doi:10.1177/0271121415594925

Snyder, P., Hemmeter, M. L., & McLaughlin, T. (2011). Professional development in early childhood intervention: Where we stand on the silver anniversary of PL 99-457. *Journal of Early Intervention, 33*, 357–370. doi:10.1177/1053815111428336

Snyder, P., Hemmeter, M. L., McLean, M. E., Sandall, S. R., & McLaughlin, T. (2013). Embedded instruction to support early learning in response to intervention frameworks. In V. Buysse & E. S. Peisner-Feinberg (Eds.), *Handbook of response to intervention in early childhood* (pp. 283–298). Baltimore, MD: Paul H. Brookes.

Snyder, P., Hemmeter, M. L., McLean, M., Sandall, S., McLaughlin, T., & Algina, J. (2018). Effects of professional development on preschool teachers' use of embedded instruction practices. *Exceptional Children, 84*, 213–232. doi:10.1177/0014402917735512

5

Collaboration in Child Care Settings
Using Teaming to Support Infants and Toddlers With Disabilities

Jenna M. Weglarz-Ward
University of Nevada, Las Vegas

Madison is an 18-month-old who loves to sing songs, "read the mail," and play with anything squishy. Because her parents work full time, Madison attends Friends of Faith child care program at her church three days each week and spends two days per week with her grandfather at his house. A few weeks ago, Toni, Madison's primary child care provider, talked to Madison's family about seeking a referral for Part C early intervention (EI) services because she thought Madison's loco-motion and balance skills were delayed, which might be impacting her ability to play with others. Based on Toni's recommendation, Madison's family began the EI process and developed an Individual Family Service Plan (IFSP) and outcomes to facilitate Madison's motor and social development. They selected Alex, a physical therapist, to begin services in the natural environment. Because Madison spends most of her time during the week out of the home with other caregivers, the family asked for services to be provided, in part, at her child care center.

Alex typically provides services in family homes but occasionally visits family and center-based child care programs. Often when he provides services in child care centers, he is unsure how to approach the situation because each program has different environments, schedules, and staff. He would like to provide services within the typical routines of the child care program, using their materials and involving child care providers and other children. However, some programs have asked him to provide services outside the classroom so they won't distract the other children.

Toni had not heard anything from Madison's family about EI since that meet-ing a few weeks ago. However yesterday, Madison's dad mentioned that a physical therapist would be coming for a visit the next day. Toni had seen other therapists come to her center, but she had not worked with one herself and was not sure exactly what a physical therapist might want to do with Madison and how she could be involved in her EI services.

It has become more common for infants and toddlers with disabilities to receive their Individuals With Disabilities Education Act Part C EI services across multiple settings, including child care programs (Hebbeler, Spiker, Morrison, & Mallik, 2008; U.S. Department of Education, 2015), making child care programs natural environments for many infants and toddlers. Natural environments include settings that infants and toddlers without disabilities would experience, including family homes, child care programs, and other community settings. As Keilty (2001) notes, "the philosophy of natural environments starts with identifying where the child spends time, then addressing the developmental concerns during those everyday happenings that occur within the setting, [and] embedding interventions into family routines" (p. 32).

Providing EI services in child care programs aligns with key principles of EI that emphasize providing meaningful interventions with familiar people, settings, and materials (U.S. Department of Education, 2008). Child care programs provide opportunities for young children with disabilities to interact with peers without disabilities while also fostering learning across all domains of development and supporting parents' efforts to seek out work, schooling, or rest from parenting (Shonkoff & Phillips, 2000; Wall, Kisker, Peterson, Carta, & Jeon, 2006). Furthermore, including very young children with disabilities in community-based programs such as child care promotes a sense of belonging for these children and families (DEC/NAEYC, 2009; U.S. Department of Health and Human Services & U.S. Department of Education [U.S. DHHS/DOE], 2015). By providing access to programs, enhancing their participation, and supporting families and professionals to coordinate services across natural environments, inclusion for infants and toddlers can be achieved.

Collaborations among early childhood professionals are essential to high-quality inclusion and positive child and family outcomes (Dinnebeil, Buysse, Rush, & Eggbeer, 2008; Guillen & Winton, 2015; U.S. DHHS/DOE, 2015). Collaboration is a dynamic relationship in which people pool their collective expertise to achieve mutually agreed upon goals (DEC, 2014; Guillen & Winton, 2015). Systematic and regular teaming efforts build the capacity of each team member, including families, to problem solve as well as plan and implement interventions. However, collaboration, particularly with professionals from different disciplines, is challenging. Often professionals lack the time to build the necessary relationships with each other to effectively meet the needs of the children and their families (Weglarz-Ward, 2016; Wesley, Buysse, & Skinner, 2001).

The purpose of this article is to provide insight into the benefits and challenges of collaboration among child care and EI providers (e.g., occupational therapists, physical therapists, special instructors, service coordinators, speech-language pathologists) when supporting infants and toddlers with disabilities as well as to discuss strategies that enhance professional collaboration. This article will examine the importance of building foundational knowledge of different programs and disciplines (TC1), how to engage in joint planning (TC2), and ways to facilitate effective communication (TC3). We will learn about the journey Toni and Alex take to build an effective collaboration to promote Madison's development and inclusion in her center-based child care program.

Building Foundational Knowledge Across Child Care and EI

When Alex arrived at Friends of Faith, he signed in as a visitor, asked which classroom to go to, and headed down the hall. He smiled as he saw the artwork on the walls and the children finishing up lunch at the toddler-sized tables and chairs. He introduced himself to Toni, who was helping two children wash their hands, and told her he was there to see Madison. Toni looked at the clock and realized that it was almost naptime, but she did not want to interfere with the EI plan. She told him Madison had finished eating and was over in the library reading some books with another staff member. Alex moved over to the library area and asked Madison if she wanted to play with him. She smiled and took his hand. Alex was delighted to see a small loft area with stairs and a slide in the room, so he decided to take her over there. As Alex and Madison played at the stairs and she slid down the slide, a few other children went to join them. Toni and the other staff moved them away saying, "That is Madison's special teacher, and they need to do some work right now." Alex overheard this and was not sure whether he could involve Madison's peers in the session. Toni continued to clean up from lunch and prepare for nap while also trying to watch Alex and Madison so she could do some of the same things once he left. After some songs and dancing, Alex brought Madison over to Toni and said the visit went well. He mentioned that Toni could try to have her use the stairs more and he would be back next week. He wrote a note and put it in Madison's backpack. After he left, Toni sat with Madison in the rocking chair and read books quietly through nap time.

In early childhood, professionals across many disciplines work together to plan and implement services for infants and toddlers with disabilities and their families (TC1). Although both child care and EI programs foster the development and learning of young children, they may use different approaches and service delivery models. For example, child care programs focus on group instruction, provide daily care as well as educational opportunities, and address child learning across all domains of development. Child care providers are typically experts on that child, family, and the routines and interactions that occur at child care. EI programs, on the other hand, provide individualized intervention, target services related to child and family outcomes, and may focus on specific domains

> Although both child care and early intervention programs foster the development and learning of young children, they may use different approaches and service delivery models.

of development. EI providers are experts on the EI process and intervention strategies specific to their discipline. In developing a collaborative relationship, professionals can first learn about and respect each other's experience, expertise, and contributions to child learning. Additionally, by learning about each other's programs, professionals are able to coordinate services across programs.

Supporting child care providers' knowledge. One area where child care providers may need support is in understanding the EI process (i.e., referral, evaluation, planning, implementation, transition), the legislation and policies that support inclusion (e.g., IDEA and the Americans With Disabilities Act), the roles and expertise of EI specialists (e.g., physical therapy, occupational therapy, applied behavioral analysis), and EI structures (e.g., agency-based, independent contractors, and state-based providers). Child care providers have reported they learn about EI through the providers that visit their programs (Weglarz-Ward, Santos, & Timmer, 2018), suggesting that EI providers take time to discuss or provide resources on the EI process and what EI visits may look like. This includes explaining EI key principles and routines-based intervention so child care providers can understand the value of providing services within the child care setting with the available materials and with other children in the classroom. In Madison's case, Toni thought that allowing other children to interact with Madison during Alex's visit would detract from services when, in fact, it might have helped reinforce Alex accomplishing her outcomes and her sense of belonging in the program. In addition to discussions with the teaching staff, EI providers can provide books, articles, and online resources on disability, child development, and evidence-based practices to support children with disabilities.

Supporting EI providers' knowledge. As early childhood services vary in structure, it is important for EI providers to learn about different child care programs (e.g., family-based, center-based, faith related) and models of delivery (e.g., primary caregiving, looping, mixed aged) as well as the staffing structures (e.g., directors, co-teachers, master teachers, assistants, floaters). This includes learning about commonly used curricula or philosophies (e.g., Creative Curriculum, emergent-curriculum, Montessori, Pyramid Model) and program policies (e.g., visitor procedures, developmentally appropriate materials, food restrictions, and health and safety protocols). EI providers may ask for a copy of the program's handbook, inclusion policy, and planning and teaming procedures, or they may benefit from reviewing program and state licensing and Quality Rating and Improvement System (QRIS) standards.

Speaking with the director or owner of the child care program allows EI providers to understand the program and plan EI visits accordingly. McWilliam (2011) cautions EI professionals from working with children one-on-one or outside the classroom because it limits the child care providers' feeling of being a part of the EI process and minimizes intergration of familiar people, materials, and routines. To provide these meaningful routine-based interventions, EI providers could learn about each programs' daily schedule, the staff that they will be interacting with, and possible special events or thematic units that might influence the child care environment. For example, Alex came to the program during the transition from lunch to naptime, which was not an optimal time for gross motor activity, and it prevented Madison from resting that day. Determining

> In developing a collaborative relationship, professionals can first learn about and respect each other's experience, expertise, and contributions to child learning.

Madison's preferences and the daily routines with Toni before his initial visit would allow Alex to plan his visits during a free-choice period, gym time, or outdoor play because gross motor activities are likely to naturally occur during these times. If the program is focusing time on learning about animals, for example, he could incorporate animal-themed movements or songs into his sessions.

Addressing professional development and training. Although professionals often receive training in special education and different instructional and therapeutic practices, they rarely receive formal training in collaboration (Mulvihill, Shearer, & Van Horn, 2002; Weglarz-Ward, 2016; Wesley et al., 2001). Therefore, it is important for both child care and EI providers to focus on learning about teaming and collaboration, including understanding the multiple disciplines providing services to the child (Allen & Kelly, 2015). It is beneficial for all providers to receive personnel preparation and professional development specific to teaming, including differences between multidisciplinary, interdisciplinary, and transdisciplinary teams as well as strategies for consultation and coaching

(Dinnebeil et al., 2008). In addition to coursework, supervised fieldwork, and live trainings, free open-access, online professional development resources such as *CONNECT Module 3: Communication for Collaboration* (Winton, Buysse, Turnbull, & Rous, 2010) provide opportunities for faculty and professional development providers, such as coaches and supervisors, to support professional learning using hybrid approaches (i.e., facilitated learning using online resources). Consideration of licensure requirements and continuing education credits for these learning experiences from state leaders may encourage professional participation.

Additionally, creating opportunities for professionals from child care and EI to come together supports collaboration. This can be done through professional development, cross-disciplinary communities of practice, or providers doing in-house trainings at different programs (e.g., an occupational therapist speaking at a child care's monthly staff meeting, a state child care administrator visiting an EI office to share current licensure activities). The Early Intervention Training Program at the University of Illinois (2015) has developed a live training, "Natural Partners in Natural Environments," that is approved by both the child care and EI systems for contining education credits. It invites providers to learn from each other through guided activities in teaming, communication, and conflict resolution. Child care and EI providers could also form virtual or live communities of practice to share their expertise, problem solve, and support each other. For example, family and center-based providers and EI providers in the same geographic neighborhood could meet once per month at a local library or

Table 1

Considerations When Planning and Implementing EI Services in Child Care Settings

- EI state and program policies on information sharing and liability should be reviewed.
- Families must provide written consent to share information between child care and EI providers. Consider that confidential EI information includes outcomes, IFSP documents, and contact notes. Confidential information should not be discussed in front of other children and families.
- Depending on state policies, child care directors, owners, and providers may not be formal IFSP team members. Child care professionals may be invited by the family to attend IFSP meetings.
- EI providers may need to undergo verification processes (i.e., background checks, fingerprinting, tuberculous testing) to provide services within a child care program.
- EI providers may not be able to be alone with children while providing services at a child care program.
- Consider developing formal memorandums of understandings (MOUs) between child care and EI programs to outline clear expectations, responsibilities, activities, and program accountability.

For resources, see Early Intervention Training Program at the University of Illinois (2015) and Washington State Department of Health Children with Special Health Care Needs Program (2012).

coffee shop or set up a private social media page to ask each other questions and share interesting articles and professional resources. These joint opportunities provide access to consistent content as well as build relationships among professionals.

Joint Planning Among Child Care and EI

Planning among all the key players for a child receiving EI services is vital to plan and provide appropriate interventions for a child during daily routines (TC2). Like Toni, child care providers are not often involved in the planning of IFSP outcomes or strategies. This leads to uncertainty between child care and EI providers on how to involve each other in their work (McWilliam, 2011). It's important to develop policies and procedures to include child care providers in planning so they can support the children's learning and communicate to families about EI visits at child care and progress toward achieving child outcomes. Formal agreements such as memorandums of understanding outlining specific expectations, responsibilities, and accountability are beneficial. There are some important aspects to consider when planning across programs (see Table 1), most notably understanding legal aspects of confidentiality and liability. With an understanding of the necessary procedures and *with family permission*, child care providers could be important members of IFSP teams, providing information about the child's interactions with peers and their skills during child care routines as well as contributing to IFSP outcomes and problem-solving any issues with the team as they implement the plan.

Administrators such as center directors, program owners, service coordinators, and program managers play key roles in collaboration (see Table 2). Researchers have concluded that a clearly articulated philosophy on inclusion supports practices, such as those recommended by DEC (2014), including collaboration among professionals (Devore & Hanley-Maxwell, 2000; Wong & Cumming, 2010). Using teaming checklists, administrators can reflect on their current perspectives and plan future actions (see Early Childhood Technical Assistance Center, n.d.; Rush & Shelden, 2012 for examples of checklists). Therefore, administrators can develop a philosophy and practices that support collaborative planning such as having flexible work hours, substitute staff, and creative communication (e.g., virtual meetings). Additionally, professional development on disability-related topics, including collaboration, is essential (Mulvihill et al., 2002). This is particularly important when teaming with home-based programs that may lack additional staffing and resources to allow staff to attend meetings during the day (Weglarz-Ward, 2016; Wong & Cumming, 2010).

All providers need to work closely with each other to establish clear expectations and intentionally plan their roles during each stage of the EI process. (See Table 3 for explanation of roles for different programs at each stage of referral, evaluation, and service delivery.) EI providers should not assume that child care providers understand how to carry over intervention strategies throughout their daily routines. However, discussing this expectation at the beginning of the relationship will set a foundation for successful routine-based strategies and help structure communication and implementation. Furthermore, as recommended by McWilliam (2015), EI providers may use coaching strategies to help child care providers learn how to support children's outcomes.

As Alex finished up his notes about Madison's visit, he thought about how kind the child care providers were to him even though the classroom was busy. Toni cared greatly for Madison and wanted to observe more of Alex's visit, but she was not sure how to do that. On his way out, he noticed the classroom schedule on the door and noted it for his next visit. As he signed out of the visitor log, he left his card with the center director and mentioned that he was going to speak with his supervisor on strategies for including Toni during his visits if that was okay.

Table 2

Considerations of Administrators in Planning and Implementing EI Services in Child Care Settings

- Be willing to be creative and take risks to team with other professionals.
- Consider your program philosophy and how this includes children with disabilities and collaboration with professionals across disciplines.
- Develop policies for sharing confidential information with families, child care, and EI professionals.
- Provide time, compensation, and technology for teaming activities, including attending IFSP meetings, joint planning time, and communication.
- Be flexible in your scheduling to reflect the needs of child care, EI professionals, and families. This includes scheduling teaming activities early in the morning or evening or during rest time.
- Support professional development activities for staff specific to collaboration, including time and financial support to attend trainings, conferences, and online opportunities.
- Actively build relationships with other child care and EI programs to share resources. Invite providers from child care and EI to staff meetings or trainings.

For resources, see Child Care Aware, Division for Early Childhood, and The Ounce (2017), Early Childhood Technical Assistance Center (n.d.), Rush and Shelden (2012), U.S. Department of Health and Human Services and U.S. Department of Education (2015), and Winton, Buysse, Turnbull, and Rous (2010).

Table 3
Roles and Expectations During the Early Intervention Process

Program	Screening	Referral	Evaluation	Service delivery
Head Start/ Early Head Start	A program must complete or obtain a current vision, hearing, and developmental screening within 45 calendar days of when the child first attends the program or within 30 calendar days for programs that operate for 90 days or less.	Programs must make a referral to the local agency responsible for implementing IDEA. Referral is based on results of screening as well as additional relevant information and with direct guidance from a mental health or child development professional. Referral must be made with parental consent.	If a child is determined to be eligible for services under IDEA, the program must partner with parents and the local agency responsible for implementing IDEA, as appropriate, and deliver the services required to ensure full participation in all program activities.	Regulatory mandate states that a minimum of 10% of enrollment must be children with disabilities.
Child care	Child Care and Development Fund (CCDF) requires that lead agencies provide consumer education about developmental screenings to parents, the general public, and, when applicable, child care providers. It strongly recommends that lead agencies develop strategies to ensure all children receive a research-based developmental and behavioral screening within 45 days of enrollment, which aligns with Head Start standards.	There is variation across states.	Teachers can participate in IFSPs and IEPs if requested by parents.	Children with disabilities have the right to attend community-based child care through the Americans with Disabilities Act of 1990. A lead agency could include in its eligibility determination process a question about whether the child has an IEP or IFSP so the parent could be provided with information on which child care provider would best meet the child's individual needs.

Table 3 (continued)
Roles and Expectations During the Early Intervention Process

Program	Screening	Referral	Evaluation	Service delivery
Early intervention (IDEA Part C)	States must have child find activities in place to identify, locate, and evaluate infants and toddlers with disabilities.	Referrals are coordinated through local early intervention service providers.	Local early intervention service providers must conduct a comprehensive evaluation within 45 days of receiving parental consent.	If an infant or toddler is eligible for services, the IFSP team develops an IFSP.
Preschool special education (IDEA Part B, Section 619)	States must have child find activities in place to identify, locate, and evaluate preschool children with disabilities.	Local educational agencies coordinate referrals.	Local educational agencies must conduct an evaluation within 60 days (or within state established timelines) of receiving parental consent.	If a child is eligible for services, the IEP team develops an IEP.
Parents	Parents can request a developmental screening at any time if they are concerned about their child's development.	Parents can contact local IDEA programs at any time to request an evaluation if they are concerned with their child's development.	Parents participate in the assessment and evaluation process. Parents have due process rights under IDEA.	Parents are members of the team that develops their child's IFSP or IEP.

From "Partnerships for inclusion: Ensuring access to high quality evaluations and services," by S. Parikshak, C. Kavulic, P. Winton, and J. M. Eile, n.d. Webinar presented by the National Center on Early Childhood Development, Teaching, and Learning and the Early Childhood Technical Assistance Center. Retrieved from https://eclkc.ohs.acf. hhs.gov/video/partnerships-inclusion-ensuring-access-high-quality-evaluation-services

At the end of the day, Toni spoke with Madison's dad about Alex's visit. She said that Madison seemed to enjoy the visit and Alex left a note about the visit in her backpack. Toni then said that she would like to assist with Madison's EI plan implementation. Upon a suggestion from her director, Toni recommended that they ask the IFSP team for some ideas about how to do that and get back to her. Later that week, the Friends of Faith director spoke with Madison's parents and service coordinator. The family completed the necessary paperwork to share Madison's IFSP with Toni and the other staff and set up a meeting to talk through the plan with Madison's family and Alex and jointly problem-solve any barriers to implementation.

Effective Communication Between Child Care and EI

Communication is key in any relationship. For collaboration to be successful, team members need to be intentional about their communication (TC3). Often child care and EI providers communicate at the beginning or the end of a visit. Although this may help to build a relationship, these brief interactions may not be functional long term. For example, like many child care providers, Toni may be doing multiple things at once, such as answering questions from a curious toddler while she cleans the snack table and scanning the room after hearing a shout. It is difficult for Toni to have a meaningful conversation with Alex about any of Madison's celebrations or concerns. Furthermore, Alex schedules sessions throughout the day and must leave quickly after Madison's session to drive through traffic to get to his next EI visit on time. Finding a time that both providers can focus on consultation will be important to their collaboration.

In a recent study with child care and EI providers, EI providers felt as if they were communicating often and clearly, but child care providers reported receiving significantly less communication (Weglarz-Ward, 2016). For example, EI providers often reported that they would always leave a contact note after the visit and assumed child care providers would read the note and understand the expectations between visits. Child care providers, on the other hand, reported not even knowing there was a note. These findings indicate that an explicit communication plan is needed. Additionally, as the child care provider is often not asked to be part of the IFSP team, all communication about that child's services is confidential (including contact notes) and families must consent to this release of information. Therefore, EI providers could take time to develop a communication strategy including obtaining permission from families, setting aside time to talk with child care providers before and after EI visits, and being creative about modes of communication (e.g., e-mail, phone calls). Additionally, it would be helpful to identify a primary team member from child care (i.e., director, owner, primary caregiver) and the EI program (e.g., service coordinator, primary service provider) to coordinate communication and planning efforts.

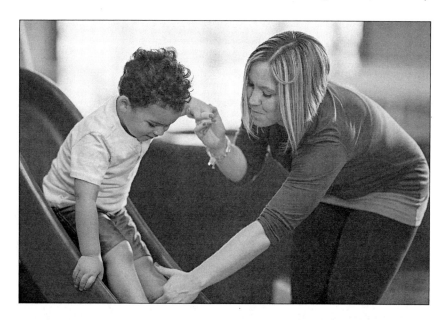

Madison has been receiving EI services for six months. For her upcoming IFSP meeting, the Friends of Faith director offered to host the meeting so she and Toni could attend and Madison's parents could see Alex's visit at the center. During the visit, Madison, who is walking with support, plays on the playground with other children. Alex models a game they have been playing and then invites Toni

and Madison's dad to join them. Afterward, they go into an empty classroom to review the IFSP. The center arranged for a substitute to step into the classroom so Toni could attend the meeting. In addition to Alex's assessment, Madison's parents share what progress they have seen at home, and Toni shares the progress she has observed at child care, particularly in Madison's play with peers. Alex again thanks Toni for sharing her lesson plans with him regularly because it helps him plan for visits. Toni notes she has learned a lot about motor development through some of the articles that Alex has shared. Using a communication notebook and videos of Alex's visits, everyone feels that Madison is well supported throughout her daily routines both at home and child care and is making great gains.

As children with disabilities receiving services in child care programs continue to become more common, teaming among child care and EI staff helps to meaningfully include very young children with disabilities in their natural environments. However, teaming with other professionals is more than being in the same place at the same time—even with the same perceived goals (Friend & Cook, 2009). As researchers have consistently concluded, inclusive environments support positive outcomes not only for children with identified disabilities but also for those without by increasing awareness and referral of specialized services by child care providers and families and the implementation of needed individualized supports and evidence-based practices (Devore & Hanley-Maxwell, 2000, Mulvihill et al., 2002; U.S. DHHS/DOE, 2015).

To improve the early childhood workforce and quality services for young children, we need to strengthen collaboration and communication among professionals across early education and care services (Allen & Kelly, 2015). Therefore, intentional steps may be taken to ensure that EI and child care staff have knowledge of the different early childhood services (TC1); that they have time to plan and problem-solve across these services, which often have strict policies and procedures (TC2); and that they develop functional communication systems among already busy professionals (TC3). Effective steps in these areas build strong collaborations. In turn, collaboration among child care and EI providers promotes high-quality inclusion and positive outcomes for infants and toddlers with disabilities and their families.

References

Allen, L., & Kelly, B. B. (Eds.). (2015). *Transforming the workforce for children birth through age 8: A unifying foundation.* Washington DC: National Academies Press.

DEC/NAEYC. (2009). *Early childhood inclusion: A joint position statement of the Division for Early Childhood (DEC) and the National Association for the Education of Young Children (NAEYC).* Chapel Hill, NC: FPG Child Development Institute.

DeVore, S., & Hanley-Maxwell, C. (2000). "I wanted to see if we could make it work": Perspectives on inclusive childcare. *Exceptional Children, 66,* 241–255. doi:10.1177/001440290006600208

Dinnebeil, L., Buysse, V., Rush, D., & Eggbeer, L. (2008). Becoming effective collaborators and change agents. In P. J. Winton, J. A. McCollum, & C. Catlett (Eds.), *Practical approaches to early childhood professional development: Evidence, strategies, and resources* (pp. 227–245). Washington DC: Zero to Three Press.

Division for Early Childhood. (2014). *DEC recommended practices for early intervention/early childhood special education 2014*. Retrieved from http://www.dec-sped.org/dec-recommended-practices

Early Childhood Technical Assistance Center. (n.d.). *RP products by topic: Teaming and collaboration*. Retrieved from http://ectacenter.org/decrp/topic-teaming.asp

Early Intervention Training Program at the University of Illinois. (2015, March 11). *Early intervention and child care... natural partners in natural environments*. Retrieved from https://blogs.illinois.edu/view/6039/230963#CC

Friend, M., & Cook, L. (2009). *Interactions: Collaboration skills for school professionals* (6th ed.). Boston, MA: Pearson Education.

Guillen, C., & Winton, P. (2015). Teaming and collaboration: Thinking about how as well as what. In Division for Early Childhood, *DEC recommended practices: Enhancing services for young children with disabilities and their families* (DEC Recommended Practices Monograph Series No. 1; pp. 99–108). Los Angeles, CA: Division for Early Childhood.

Hebbeler, K., Spiker, D., Morrison, K., & Mallik, S. (2008). A national look at the characteristics of Part C early intervention services. In C. A. Peterson, L. Fox, & P. M. Blasco (Eds.), *Early intervention for infants and toddlers and their families: Practices and outcomes* (Young Exceptional Children Monograph Series No. 10; pp. 1–18). Missoula, MT: Division for Early Childhood.

Keilty, B. (2001). Are natural environments worth it? Using a cost-benefit framework to evaluate early intervention policies in community programs. *Infants & Young Children, 13*, 32–43.

McWilliam, R. (2011). The top 10 mistakes in early intervention in natural environments and the solutions. *Zero to Three, 31*(4), 11–16.

McWilliam, R. A. (2015). Future of early intervention with infants and toddlers for whom typical experiences are not effective. *Remedial and Special Education, 36*, 33–38. doi:10.1177/0741932514554105

Mulvihill, B. A., Shearer, D., & Van Horn, M. L. (2002). Training, experience, and child care providers' perceptions of inclusion. *Early Childhood Research Quarterly, 17*, 197–215. doi:10.1016/S0885-2006(02)00145-X

Parikshak, S., Kavulic, C., Winton, P., & Eile, J. M. (n.d.). *Partnerships for inclusion: Ensuring access to high quality evaluations and services*. Webinar presented by the National Center on Early Childhood Development, Teaching, and Learning and the Early Childhood Technical Assistance Center. Retrieved from https://eclkc.ohs.acf.hhs.gov/video/partnerships-inclusion-ensuring-access-high-quality-evaluation-services

Rush, D. D., & Shelden, M. L. (2012). Checklists for providing/receiving early intervention supports in child care settings. *Casetools, 6*(1).

Shonkoff, J. P., & Phillips, D. A. (2000). *From neurons to neighborhoods: The science of early childhood development.* Washington, DC: National Academy Press.

U.S. Department of Education, Office of Special Education and Rehabilitative Services. (2015). *37th annual report to Congress on the implementation of the Individuals With Disabilities Education Act, 2015.* Washington, DC: Author.

U.S. Department of Education, Office of Special Education Programs (OSEP) TA Community of Practice: Part C Settings. (2008, March). *Agreed upon mission and key principles for providing early intervention services in natural environments.* Retrieved from http://ectacenter.org/~pdfs/topics/families/Finalmissionandprinciples3_11_08.pdf

U.S. Department of Health and Human Services & U.S. Department of Education. (2015, September 14). *Policy statement on inclusion of children with disabilities in early childhood programs.* Retrieved from http://www2.ed.gov/policy/speced/guid/earlylearning/joint-statement-full-text.pdf

Wall, S., Kisker, E. E., Peterson, C. A., Carta, J. J., & Jeon, H. -J. (2006). Child care for low-income children with disabilities: Access, quality, and parental satisfaction. *Journal of Early Intervention, 28,* 283–298. doi:10.1177/10538151060280040410

Weglarz-Ward, J. M. (2016). *Project Collaborative Care: Experiences of child care and early intervention providers* (Doctoral dissertation). Available from ProQuest Dissertations and Theses database. (UMI No. 10609940)

Weglarz-Ward, J. M., Santos, R. M., & Timmer, J. (2018). Factors that impact inclusion in child care settings: Perspectives from child care and early intervention providers. *Early Childhood Education Journal.* Advance online publication. doi:10.1007/s10643-018-0900-3

Wesley, P. W., Buysse, V., & Skinner, D. (2001). Early interventionists' perspectives on professional comfort as consultants. *Journal of Early Intervention, 24,* 112–128. doi:10.1177/105381510102400206

Winton, P., Buysse, V., Turnbull, A., & Rous, B. (2010). *CONNECT module 3: Communication for collaboration.* Chapel Hill, NC: CONNECT: The Center to Mobilize Early Childhood Knowledge. Retrieved from http://community.fpg.unc.edu/connect-modules/learners/module-3

Wong, S., & Cumming, T. (2010). Family day care is for normal kids: Facilitators and barriers to the inclusion of children with disabilities in family day care. *Australasian Journal of Early Childhood, 35*(3), 4–12.

6

"They're Our Children"
Teaming and Collaboration Between Head Start and 619 Programs to Support Children With Disabilities in Head Start

Sarah Pedonti
Chih Ing Lim
Pamela J. Winton
University of North Carolina at Chapel Hill

Wanda Becton
WAGES Head Start

Rhonda Wiggins
Wayne County Public Schools

On the first and third Friday of each month, Wanda and Rhonda meet in Rhonda's office at the local school system to discuss Child Find referrals and collaboratively problem-solve issues confronting their respective programs. As leaders in their small rural Head Start program and Preschool Special Education Services offices, respectively, they are responsible for ensuring that their programs can effectively jointly serve the many preschool children with disabilities that reside in their district and do so in a way that includes those children in high-quality early childhood settings alongside their typically developing peers. On this particular Friday, while discussing the use of a braided funding strategy to support a blended inclusive classroom that serves both typically developing Head Start children and children with disabilities identified by the local education agency (LEA), Rhonda remarked, "You know, some people say this is your money, that's my money, but you know what? They're *our* children."

The inability to blend funding streams has been described as a frequent challenge to inclusion (Barton & Smith, 2015). Wanda and Rhonda have, however, successfully used braided funding to operate two collaborative Head Start-LEA classrooms with half the children identified as typically developing and half identified as children with disabilities. They combined both their funding sources and expertise to operate these classrooms. Head Start provides support for staff development and funding for teacher supplies, among other things, and the LEA provides the physical space and qualified teachers, as well as in-house therapists needed to work with teachers and families to meet the Individualized Education Program (IEP) goals for children with disabilities.

Rhonda and Wanda's conversation, and their efforts to braid funding, capture the spirit of quality collaboration between Head Start programs and LEAs. Head Start has historically led the way in providing inclusive settings for young children with disabilities. Through a legislative mandate passed in 1972 requiring that 10% of enrolled children have an identified disability, Head Start became the first major public education program to provide preschool children with disabilities across the nation with an inclusive educational environment. While Head Start served as the vanguard for inclusive preschool settings, many state and local preschool programs serving children with disabilities in inclusive settings now exist, and it is essential for Head Start programs to engage and collaborate with them to serve the children and families most in need of quality inclusive services.

In this article, we describe Rhonda and Wanda's interactions as a case study of a collaborative partnership between two individuals, one working in a Head Start program based in a rural county in eastern North Carolina and the other working in the LEA in that county. We examine the practices they use to support the inclusion of children with disabilities in their community and how strategies for implementing the Teaming and Collaboration recommended practices supported their successful partnership. Information on infrastructure supports that helped them develop and sustain the teaming and collaboration practices are also included.

> Collaborative adult partnerships and relationships are foundational for Head Start and LEA programs to deliver the highest quality inclusive services to children with disabilities.

Rationale for Head Start/LEA Collaboration

Congress reaffirmed the Office of Head Start's pioneering commitment to children with disabilities in the 2007 Improving Head Start for School Readiness Act and the 2016 Head Start Program Performance Standards (HSPPS; Office of Head Start, 2016), which require "the full and effective participation of all children with disabilities, including but not limited to children eligible for services under IDEA" (p. 60). Additionally, the 2016 standards require that a program "must establish ongoing collaborative relationships and partnerships with community organizations such as establishing joint agreements, procedures, or contracts and arranging for onsite delivery of services as appropriate" (p. 45). These partnerships are required to include "individuals and agencies that provide services to children with disabilities and their families, elementary schools, state preschool providers, and providers of child care services" (p. 45).

There is also broad support for collaboration in the Individuals With Disabilities Education Act (IDEA, 2004), which requires that each public agency must ensure that, "to the maximum extent appropriate, children with disabilities, including children in public or private institutions or other care facilities, are educated with children who are nondisabled" in the least restrictive environment possible. In addition, federal Race to the Top-Early Learning Challenge money has provided incentives to states to ensure early childhood systems are well coordinated across agencies, including the state educational agency and 619 preschool program that oversees LEAs' implementation of IDEA (Caron, Kendall, Wilson, & Hash, 2017).

In spite of the strong legislative support for inclusion, the extent to which young children with disabilities and their families have access to high-quality inclusive settings varies greatly from state to state. National data indicate that on average less than 50% of young children with disabilities are enrolled in inclusive settings for at least 10 hours per week and receive the majority of their services there (U.S. Department of Education, 2017). That figure has not changed substantially over the last decade, causing some to say that inclusion has stalled (Barton & Smith, 2015). Given Head Start's historic role as an inclusive setting and the strong support by both the U.S. Departments of Education and Health & Human Services for inclusion (U.S. Department of Health and Human Services & U.S. Department of Education, 2015), collaborative practices between Head Start and LEAs to support inclusion are essential for every Head Start program and LEA.

Yet, many of the Head Start staff responsible for coordinating disability services and their counterparts in school districts identify collaboration as a major challenge (Barton & Smith, 2015). The underlying differences in funding streams and federal oversight, practice standards, outcomes frameworks, and geographic organization of programs are all potential barriers that must be negotiated at local program levels (Winton, 2016). This means that the individuals in local roles must be highly skilled in collaboration and teaming practices, such as those described in the Division for Early Childhood Recommended Practices (DEC, 2014), to ensure organizational partnerships are strong.

Courtesy of Frank Porter Graham Child Development Institute

The Teaming and Collaboration recommended practices were designed to "promote and sustain collaborative adult partnerships, relationships, and ongoing interactions to ensure that programs and services achieve desired child and family outcomes and goals" (DEC, 2014, p. 15). These collaborative adult partnerships and relationships are foundational for Head Start and LEA programs to deliver the highest quality inclusive services to children with disabilities and to strengthen their respective programs' capacities to lead in the field of early childhood inclusion. While we primarily focus on the Head Start-LEA partnership, it is important to note that other stakeholders (Part C early intervention, local kindergarten and elementary special education services, and families) play crucial roles in collaborating to provide inclusive services, including, but not limited to, transition considerations.

Case Example of the Development and Implementation of Teaming and Collaboration Recommended Practices

In this section, we describe specific examples of strategies Wanda, a Head Start disabilities manager (HSDM), and Rhonda, an exceptional children's preschool coordinator (ECPC) in the LEA, use to develop and implement Teaming and Collaboration recommended practices in their partnership. These strategies are organized in terms of the infrastructure supports that help develop and sustain these practices. These supports are well grounded in the literature on implementation science, which has been broadly conceived of as the study of the facilitative and impeding processes and infrastructure necessary for sustaining quality implementation of interventions. Implementation supports or drivers, as described by Fixsen, Naoom, Blase, Friedman, and Wallace (2005; see also Halle, Metz, & Martinez-Beck, 2013), consist of three major categories: professional competencies, leadership, and organizational supports, such as structures, resources, policies, and data.

Participating in and Developing Professional Development to Support Individual and Agency Relationships

Participation in a national professional development project called SpecialQuest served as a vital relationship-building experience for Wanda and Rhonda, who were then program leaders in their community working in Early Head Start (EHS) and early intervention (EI), respectively. SpecialQuest was a project funded from 1997–2010 by the Office of Head Start to promote Head Start and community collaboration to promote inclusion (Brekken, 2011). SpecialQuest provided a context and structure for local EHS and EI team members to come together over the course of four years to plan, problem-solve, and continuously improve how they work collaboratively to support young children with disabilities and their families in inclusive EHS settings.

Not only did SpecialQuest create an explicit context for multidisciplinary teaming, it also facilitated the development of EHS and EI interpersonal relationships. Through their participation in SpecialQuest, Rhonda and Wanda built their expertise with concepts related to early childhood inclusion and strengthened their leadership capacity within their rural community in support of inclusion. This participation ultimately supported their ability to implement TC2 and coordinate their respective teams to meet child and family needs in Early Head Start.

Wanda and Rhonda were able to carry that collaboration over into their eventual employment in different roles (now Rhonda is with the LEA and Wanda is with Head Start, Early Head Start, and Early Head Start-Child Care Partnerships). For instance, under their leadership, Head Start program staff participate in professional development with LEA-employed therapists and staff at the beginning of each year. Wanda and Rhonda's initiative in setting aside the necessary time and funding for joint professional development is an example of how their leadership supports their teams to implement and sustain practices that contribute to communication and team functioning as well as inclusion.

SpecialQuest provided a context and structure for local EHS and EI team members to come together over the course of four years to plan, problem-solve, and continuously improve how they work collaboratively.

Developing and Using Communication Protocols

Rhonda and Wanda's experience at SpecialQuest supported them to effectively plan and implement other structural supports, such as communication protocols, that support teamwork. For instance, the LEA regularly reviews data from a state collaboration initiative (the NC Early Learning Network) to understand the proportion of Child Find notifications coming from partners such as Head Start and to promote dialogue in improving those notification rates and ensuring timely identification of and service delivery for children with disabilities. Wanda and Rhonda meet regularly with each other's respective staffs to discuss any problems in referrals and evaluations, and they use data-based decision making to develop solutions to these issues. During these meetings, they not only model collaboration, they also facilitate team members in sharing information and brainstorming solutions to challenges, in keeping with TC3.

Another type of communication protocol implemented through the Head Start-LEA partnership is a therapy log originally developed by Wanda and later adapted to align with a previous iteration developed by the LEA. This tool supports practitioners in implementing TC2. The Head Start program and LEA therapists use the therapy log to document and record children's progress and to monitor therapists' use of inclusive service-delivery techniques, including hours of service, the setting for delivery of services (one-on-one, group, or push-in), and the type of service (direct or consultation). This builds the team's capacity for implementing interventions and solving problems at the

program level as well as at the individual child level. After therapists document their services, they share the log with Head Start teachers, who use the objectives set and successful therapeutic strategies shared by therapists to individualize their classroom lesson plans. The logs also provide a formal mechanism for therapists to offer consultative expertise to the teaching staff on children's progress beyond their direct contact with children. In this manner, the Head Start program and LEA merge multiple streams of expertise for the benefit of the child.

At the organizational level, Wanda and Rhonda jointly review therapy logs to monitor compliance and progress, reflect on rates of inclusive service provision, and further develop LEA-provided therapists' competencies for working in inclusive settings through professional development and training. If there are particular practices that therapists use during therapy sessions with the child, Wanda and Rhonda use facilitative supervision to support the therapists in coaching teachers toward embedding those practices in Head Start classrooms. This ensures that Head Start teachers get the assistance they need to learn about and implement classrom strategies to support the child's IEP goals. Depending on rates of inclusive service delivery reflected in the logs, Wanda may then co-facilitate professional development on embedding service delivery in natural routines for the LEA therapists and service providers as well as for teaching staff.

Finally, classroom teachers share therapy logs with families to discuss the services delivered and the child's progress. This provides a system of "checks and balances" to document that services are delivered as described in the IEP, and it helps the family monitor their child's progress and communicate with the teacher directly about effective strategies for meeting their child's goals.

Delineating Roles and Responsibilities for Serving Children With Disabilities and Their Families

One of the challenges identified by practitioners as having an impact on HS-LEA collaboration is the confusion of roles and responsibilities for providing services for children with disabilities and their families (National Center on Early

Courtesy of Frank Porter Graham Child Development Institute

Childhood Development, Teaching and Learning & Early Childhood Technical Assistance Center, 2016). Wanda and Rhonda encountered this confusion when they first built their collaborative partnership. Through meetings with staff and a formalized memorandum of understanding (MOU) between Head Start and the LEA, they have delineated roles and responsibilities between LEA staff (ECPC, therapists, case managers, members of the evaluation team) and Head Start staff (teachers, managers, HSDM), starting with screening, referral, and evaluation and including IEP development and implementa-

tion. For Wanda and Rhonda, the MOU hasn't been just a piece of paper that's kept in a drawer and reviewed every few years, it's become a roadmap for their collaboration. The following examples from their MOU outline each agency's responsibilities and expectations for screening and referrals:

- Head Start is responsible for screening as part of its obligations under the HSPSS and, as HSDM, Wanda consolidates the Head Start teaching staff's observations to develop complete information for the initial referral.
- The LEA also completes screenings to determine the need for evaluation. Rhonda, as the ECPC, uses the results from Head Start screenings and observations to contribute a complete picture of the child's strengths and reasons for referral.
- Additionally, the Head Start Performance Standards require hearing and vision screenings. The LEA requires hearing and vision screenings as well to complete a child's initial eligibility determination. To reduce

duplication, Rhonda relies on Head Start staff to provide the hearing and vision screenings as part of the notification to Child Find.

- Wanda is routinely invited to the child's initial referral meeting to provide insight about the teacher observations and initial screening results.

This delineation of roles and responsibilities helps each agency team share information about children as well as coordinate around planning and implementing supports and services for children and families, supporting TC2.

Leveraging Community Connections and Resources

Another way Rhonda and Wanda exchange and use information to better collaborate and build team capacity (TC2) is through their participation with community partners on their local interagency coordinating council (LICC). The goals of the LICC are to support counties in interagency partnerships and information sharing, collaboratively develop and disseminate Child Find information, and support families in early intervention (North Carolina Department of Health and Human Services, n.d.). The LICC in Wanda and Rhonda's county is active and holds regular meetings. The community partners in their county include a local pediatrician's office, representatives from their state public health program for at-risk children, representatives from early intervention, and exceptional children's coordinators from the school district. The local pediatrician has served as a long-time champion for inclusive early childhood programs and has been a driving force behind the promotion of early childhood education in their community. Wanda and Rhonda view his leadership as especially important in rallying community resources and promoting positive attitudes toward collaboration around inclusion. Wanda and Rhonda's relationships with him and other LICC members help transcend logistical barriers to solve problems.

Additionally, Wanda's and Rhonda's participation on the LICC allows them to effectively implement TC4. The LICC provides a formal way for Wanda and Rhonda to connect with other community agencies that may offer resources to benefit the families they serve and provides a way for those agencies to learn about their services. For instance, Wanda and Rhonda conduct annual mini-orientations for LICC members and their respective staff to raise community awareness of the inclusive preschool services offered by Head Start and the LEA. This has supported staff from all agencies to easily make referrals and connect families to the appropriate providers. In addition, both programs use a resource guide—initially developed using community grant funding obtained by the local pediatrician—to help practiners link families with resources in their county. They share the guide during routine encounters with families, including screening, evaluation, eligibility determination, and transition meetings. This orients families to community resources such as child care subsidies, early intervention, and mental health resources.

> This delineation of roles and responsibilities helps each agency team share information about children as well as coordinate around planning and implementing supports and services for children and families.

Conclusion

The examples from one case study of a HS-LEA partnership provide practical insight into the "on the ground" strategies and practices associated with teamwork and collaboration that helped fuel one community's journey toward providing high-quality inclusive options for children with disabilities and their families. A limitation of this particular case study is that it is not necessarily representative of all HS-LEA partnerships. For instance, this Head Start program has only one LEA partner with whom to collaborate in the county. However, a typical Head Start program collaborates on average with five LEAs (Office of Head Start, 2018). Obviously collaborating with more LEAs will complicate building partnerships, and anecdotal evidence verifies that Head Start program relationships with LEAs can vary based on a number of factors such as personalities, turnover, and available LEA resources. In spite of this caveat, there are important lessons to learn from this case study.

One lesson is that implementation "drivers" such as professional development, infrastructure supports, resources, and leadership play an important role not only in developing partnerships but also in growing and sustaining them. For example, the SpecialQuest professional development opportunity launched

a partnership between Early Head Start and early intervention. That partnership generalized more broadly to the Head Start program and the LEA, in part because two individuals carried the teaming and collaboration values and practices as well as their interpersonal relationship into their new roles in Head Start and the LEA. Their partnership, in turn, spawned local HS-LEA collaborative professional development efforts that became institutionalized as an ongoing "driver" associated with the implementation of high-quality inclusion practices.

Likewise, the LICC and MOU structures preexisted Wanda and Rhonda's partnership. As a result of their partnership, those structures were strengthened and continue to serve as "drivers" in supporting the community's inclusion efforts by clearly delineating roles and responsibilities of each partner. Tools such as therapy logs were adapted to the HS-LEA context and have also become institutionalized as ways of communicating across agencies, disciplines, and families. The pediatrician's leadership in their community as a "champion of all children" was described as important in setting the stage for communitywide buy-in to inclusion. Inspired by a champion and prepared by SpecialQuest, Wanda and Rhonda emerged as leaders of inclusion who are now supporting others to participate in building quality inclusive options in their county.

Their leadership not only supports teaming and collaboration in their agencies but embodies the spirit of the Leadership recommended practices as well. In essence, this case study is an example of how success can breed success. Implementation of the Teaming and Collaboration recommended practices at the individual leadership level can build collaboration and teamwork at the program and community levels and can sustain and grow the infrastructure supports that ensure inclusion and teamwork continue beyond the tenures of individual champions. This will not happen by chance.

What follows are three recommendations for systematic and intentional actions at community, state, regional, and national levels that can help jump start the momentum for building more high-quality inclusive options for young children with disabilities and their families across the country.

- Provide HS and LEA managers with joint leadership and professional development opportunities that build their skills and knowledge on using the Teaming and Collaboration recommended practices to support the implementation of high-quality inclusion.
- Provide HS and LEA front-line staff with sustained high-quality professional development opportunities to develop their confidence and competence in implementing all of the DEC Recommended Practices, including those for teaming and collaboration, and provide ongoing support for implementing the practices in classrooms and with families.
- Assess and improve infrastructure supports for HS and LEA managers, front-line staff, other community partners, and families to problem solve about barriers to inclusion, jointly create solutions to those challenges, and engage in practices such as the DEC Recommended Practices that support each child and families' desired outcomes for a fully inclusive life.

Without this level of support from community programs and staff, children with disabilities and their families will continue to have uneven opportunities and options for experiencing high-quality inclusion.

> Implementation "drivers" such as professional development, infrastructure supports, resources, and leadership play an important role not only in developing partnerships but also in growing and sustaining them.

References

Barton, E. E., & Smith, B. J. (2015). Advancing high-quality preschool inclusion: A discussion and recommendations for the field. *Topics in Early Childhood Special Education, 35*, 69–78. doi:10.1177/0271121415583048

Brekken, L. (2011). Early Head Start and early intervention: Partnerships that make a difference for young children with disabilities and their families. *Zero to Three Journal, 31*(4), 32–38.

Caron, B., Kendall, R., Wilson, G., & Hash, M. (2017, December). *Taking on the challenge: Building a strong foundation for early learning* (Early Learning Challenge Summary Report). Herndon, VA: AEM Corp.

Division for Early Childhood. (2014). *DEC recommended practices in early intervention/early childhood special education 2014*. Retrieved from http://www.dec-sped.org/dec-recommended-practices

Fixsen, D. L., Naoom, S. F., Blase, K. A., Friedman, R. M., & Wallace, F. (2005). *Implementation research: A synthesis of the literature* (FMHI Publication No. 231). Tampa: University of South Florida, Louis de la Parte Florida Mental Health Institute, The National Implementation Research Network.

Halle, T., Metz, A., & Martinez-Beck, I. (Eds.). (2013). *Applying implementation science in early childhood programs and systems.* Baltimore, MD: Paul H. Brookes.

Improving Head Start for School Readiness Act, 42 U.S.C. § 9801 (2007).

Individuals With Disabilities Education Act, 20 U.S.C. § 1400 (2004).

National Center on Early Childhood Development, Teaching and Learning & Early Childhood Technical Assistance Center. (2016). *Partnerships for inclusion: Ensuring access to high quality evaluations and services* (Series on High Quality Inclusion: Webinar 1). Retrieved from https://eclkc.ohs.acf.hhs.gov/video/partnerships-inclusion-ensuring-access-high-quality-evaluation-services

North Carolina Department of Health and Human Services. (n.d.). North Carolina infant-toddler program (NC ITP). Retrieved from https://beearly.nc.gov/index.php/icc/licc

Office of Head Start. (2016, September). *Head Start program performance standards.* Retrieved from https://eclkc.ohs.acf.hhs.gov/sites/default/files/pdf/hspps-appendix.pdf

U.S. Department of Health and Human Services & U.S. Department of Education. (2015). *Policy statement on the inclusion of children with disabilities in early childhood programs.* Retrieved from http://www2.ed.gov/policy/speced/guid/earlylearning/joint-statement-full-text.pdf

U.S. Department of Education. (2017). *Part B state performance plan/annual performance report 2017 indicator analyses.* Retrieved from https://osep.grads360.org/#communities/pdc/documents/14725

Winton, P. J. (2016). Taking stock and moving forward: Implementing quality early childhood inclusive practices. In B. Reichow, B. A. Boyd, E. E. Barton, & S. L. Odom (Eds.), *Handbook of early childhood special education* (pp. 57–74). Cham, Switzerland: Springer International.

7

Implementing Teaming and Collaboration Recommended Practices Statewide
Varying Paths Toward a Common Destination in Iowa's Part C Program

Mollie Romano
Juliann J. Woods
Florida State University

Cindy Chettinger
Northwest AEA

Heather Donoho
Des Moines Public Schools

Angie Hance
Central Rivers AEA

Jeanie Wade Nagle
Grant Wood AEA

Cindy Weigel
Melissa Schnurr
Iowa Department of Education

IF IMPLEMENTING THE TEAMING AND COLLABORATION RECOMMENDED practices for a child and family or within an early intervention program can be a challenge, then imagine the challenges when the effort is undertaken statewide. That's what Iowa is striving to do! Statewide implementation of the Division for Early Childhood (2014) Recommended Practices is a goal of Early ACCESS, Iowa's IDEA Part C System, a partnership between families with young children (birth to age 3) and early intervention providers from Iowa's Area Education Agencies (AEAs), the Iowa Departments of Education (IDOE), Public Health and Human Services, and Child Health Specialty Clinics. In Early ACCESS, families and interdisciplinary team members[1] work together to identify, coordinate, and implement services and supports that help families assist their infants and toddlers in their growth and development. Representatives of the partnership agencies use the DEC Recommended Practices to jointly develop guidelines and policy to improve child and family outcomes. They are committed to a common vision, shared decision-making based on data, and coordinated evidence-based professional development to ensure high-quality early intervention services. Early ACCESS service implementation is provided across the state through nine regional AEAs, each with local administrators and personnel. The AEAs were formed and are funded to identify and serve children birth through age 21 who require special education services to be successful in an equitable manner across the numerous large and small school districts in the state's 99 counties.

To support statewide consistency and coordination, Early ACCESS program leaders from each of the AEAs joined state-level leaders from the Iowa Departments of Education, Public Health and Human Services, and Child Health Specialty Clinics to form the Early ACCESS Leadership Group (EAGL) to guide the development and implementation of Early ACCESS services and supports. They meet about five times per year, complete needs assessments, provide input

Courtesy of Frank Porter Graham Child Development Institute

to state plans and procedures, share resources, and collaborate on the implementation of their Early ACCESS vision at the state and local levels. In 2012, the EAGL team and the IDOE initiated a professional development collaboration with Florida State University to support a shift in the delivery of services and supports to a family-guided approach. Rather than provide direct services to children, this approach supports early intervention team members to learn to coach families to embed intervention on their priority outcomes within the family's everyday routines and activities (family-guided routines-based intervention [FGRBI]; Kashinath, Woods, & Goldstein, 2006; Woods, Kashinath, & Goldstein, 2004). FGRBI emphasizes the role of family members on the team as active decision makers guiding the identification of meaningful outcomes to embed in their everyday routines and activities to support their child's learning and their family's participation. The role of the early intervention team members as coaches to the family encourages them to rethink how their interactions can build families' confidence and capacity to support their child.

During the five years of the project, each AEA identified interdisciplinary team members, including early childhood special educators, SLPs, OTs, PTs, and service coordinators—all employed by the AEA—to participate in ongoing professional development in FGRBI. Team members completing the professional development participated in monthly coaching with FSU coaches. This included viewing home visit videos, identifying coaching strategies used with families, and using problem-solving strategies to address challenges in implementing practices and reaching fidelity as a team. Team members who were trained to use FGRBI learned to use specific, measurable, and manualized key indicators of FGRBI (Marturana, McComish, Woods, & Crais, 2011; Shelden & Rush, 2013; Woods et al., 2017) as a measure of their implementation fidelity. This fidelity measure was used both as a self-assessment tool and as an observational measure completed by the external coaches and by observers from FSU. Because not all team members could participate in the professional development sequence at the same time, information about evidence-based intervention strategies and FGRBI was exchanged at team meetings to share how FGRBI supports the children and families. By 2017, almost 200 team members had completed the professional development sequence. Fifteen who were implementing FGRBI at approximately 80% fidelity received additional professional development to develop their skills as internal coaches to help others adopt and sustain the model in their region. The roles of the internal coaches include coaching assigned families during home visits, coaching other team members who have not participated in professional development, leading professional development for their agency and teams, and contributing to their regional implementation team to support sustainability. These strategies reflect what is known about successful coaching/professional development strategies to support the implementation of specific practices (Lu, 2010; Showers & Joyce, 1996).

Although Early ACCESS guidelines and policy embrace the implementation of the Teaming and Collaboration recommended practices, the shift from multidisciplinary, child-directed services to a focus on family priorities and caregiver coaching necessitated creative problem-solving and repeated efforts on how to implement the Teaming and Collaboration recommended practices in ways that accommodate the AEA's nine regional and local current practices, geography, administrative and supervisory structures, and personnel resources. The AEAs each determine the organizational structure that addresses their programs, personnel, and logistical needs; therefore, a single teaming and collaboration plan across all regions or a timeline for implementation within the AEAs was not possible. Several AEAs were already implementing program changes when the initiative began, while others had not yet initiated the practice shift but were anxious to start. While the values and vision of the Teaming and Collaboration recommended practices are maintained in each AEA, the implementation details vary.

This article explores the implementation of the Teaming and Collaboration recommended practices in vignettes and quotes from AEA representatives and examines how the recommended practices are implemented in representative programs across the state with the hope that the various plans may serve as a potential road map for other states or regions interested in undertaking a similar journey. We first describe the approach of the Des Moines Public Schools (DMPS), an urban program that supports families in the city. In the DMPS, the early childhood liaison and the multidisciplinary team members have offices in the same building, which increases their access for communication and collaboration. In contrast, our second example, Northwest AEA, encompasses the northwestern corner of the state with a small city, Sioux City, as the administrative center for a large rural area. The Northwest AEA shares the details of how it took a step-by-step approach to first implement a coaching model with its early

> The shift from multidisciplinary, child-directed services to a focus on family priorities and caregiver coaching necessitated creative problem-solving and repeated efforts on how to implement the Teaming and Collaboration recommended practices.

childhood special educators and then used that common model to move toward a primary liaison approach. Our third example, Green Hills AEA, in the southwest corner of the state, is a very large and primarily rural region with seven regional field offices for its team members. In Green Hills, like Northwest, early childhood special education teachers serve children birth to age 5 and have a common supervisor while the OTs, PTs, and SLPs generally serve children birth to 21 and have supervisors specific to their discipline. This means the PTs, OTs, and SLPs have separate disciplinary team meetings in addition to Early ACCESS team meetings. Meetings must be carefully scheduled to facilitate as much participation and as little travel as possible in addition to limiting the time away from team member school assignments.

The majority of the AEAs in Iowa are similar to Green Hills and Northwest in that they serve rural areas with multiple field offices spread throughout each region. Frequently team members serve on multiple teams, and many have additional assignments such as preschool and school-age classrooms. Specialists such as teachers for the visually or hearing impaired often serve even larger catchment areas, thus increasing the challenge for collaboration and teaming. The following three examples illustrate the unique paths to implementation of the Teaming and Collaborations recommended practices that three AEAs have taken to address their individual needs, structure, and priorities.

All Together: Des Moines Public Schools

The 22 interdisciplinary team members from the Des Moines Public Schools (DMPS) in the Heartland AEA were able to take a direct route to implementing teaming practices because of their geography, small size, and high staff retention. In 2018, they had four teams consisting of an OT, PT, SLP, and two to three teachers with access to a social worker, nurse, and hearing and vision specialist. These core team members are assigned to a "home" team and attend that team meeting weekly and attend other team meetings as needed so that they can fully address TC1: "Practitioners representing multiple disciplines and families work together as a team to plan and implement supports and services to meet the unique needs of each child and family" (DEC, 2014, p. 15). Everyone makes weekly team meetings a priority. Their internal coach (the team member with additional training and designated time to support peers in their implementation of FGRBI by providing ongoing coaching) and program administrator attend as many team meetings as possible. Teams feel a collective responsibility for serving families and speak of families as "our families," not "my child/your child." Each Individualized Family Service Plan (IFSP) is unique and has outcomes, services, and team members necessary to meet the priorities of the family. They report that TC3, using "communication and group facilitation strategies to enhance team functioning and interpersonal relationships with and among team members" (DEC, 2014, p. 15), was adopted early in the transition to the new teaming approach.

Team members follow a standard agenda adapted from *The Early Intervention Teaming Handbook* (Shelden & Rush, 2013), which is shared on the agency Google Drive prior to their weekly 90-minute meeting. To build collaboration, everyone actively participates during the meetings with team members rotating

> Teams feel a collective responsibility for serving families and speak of families as "our families," not "my child/your child."

roles such as facilitator, quality assurance regulator, FGRBI/coaching expert, and equity leader. The meeting begins by taking new referrals and assigning appropriate team members to work with new families. Updates on newer referrals are then offered, and conversations include discussions of IFSP services and outcomes. Next, team members problem-solve if a team member needs assistance with coaching support or discipline-specific help from another provider. All children in the program are reviewed at least quarterly by discussing current functioning, any new needs, and next steps on the IFSP. Team members also discuss children and families in transition from Part C and make sure they are supporting the families as they prepare to exit the program.

Recently, DMPS added a few things to its agenda to support professional development in FGRBI. For example, each team has an implementation goal related to FGRBI that it develops and monitors itself. The goals for improving teaming and service implementation include increasing the time spent reviewing sessions with families, planning and debriefing on joint visits, and having deliberate con-

versations about any changes needed on the team. Team members work together to address their goals by incorporating professional development discussions and activities that focus on the DEC Family, Instruction, or Interaction recommended practices by bringing in resources (e.g., videos, articles, outcomes to share) that they believe are useful for discussion and then identifying actions to be taken in their team meeting notes.

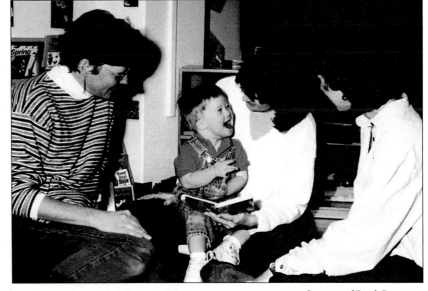

Courtesy of Frank Porter Graham Child Development Institute

Team members report that they enjoy their teaming and collaboration time and value being able to learn from one another. They also believe that this time has been instrumental in their ability to implement TC5, identifying "the primary liaison between the family and other team members based on child and family priorities and needs" (DEC, 2014, p. 15). The main provider or primary liaison serves as first contact to the family and usually sees the family weekly or every other week. Additional team members who may help address family concerns are available for the team and the family. Families know that their team has weekly meetings, and they are encouraged to share their questions or concerns so that their provider can gather support from the team and then follow up with the family. Sometimes the team member may ask to take video or pictures to share during the team meeting. Families are invited to participate by phone or video conferencing during problem-solving or quarterly updates. After meetings, team members follow up with families in person or by phone/e-mail. Sometimes a family's concern warrants a joint visit, so the primary liaison schedules a time with the family and other team members to talk about their concern.

AEAs using the primary liaison approach reported that families appreciate

Table 1
Quotes From the Family's Perspective

How did your primary liaison let you know your child had a team of other Early ACCESS providers?	"On the first visit, Stephanie gave a list of providers who were all on the team serving our family. We knew that we had access to anyone when we needed them. We were introduced to OT and SLP from the beginning of the evaluations and [they were] brought in when we needed them throughout our time in Early ACCESS. Stephanie was our teacher and primary person, and she coordinated visits and evaluations with OT and the SLP when [our child] had needs in these areas."
How did having a team of professionals available meet the needs of your child and family?	"Having a team was great. It addressed his needs of development and was met by the right person. It was perfect. They were experts in their field and came in when we needed them to help address a specific concern. Stephanie helped problem-solve by bringing that person with her on her next visit or by taking our concerns to them and addressing it with us on the next visit. Everything was coordinated and addressed at the right time, by the right person."
How did you communicate when you had a new need, concern, or question?	"We communicated at every home visit. We always talked at home visits, talked about if [we] had met a goal that we had previously been working on. We would make new goals or discuss new concerns too. Talking, texting, calling—everything was available to us to talk to our provider. Stephanie checked in with us and was always aware of his development and needs."

having a strong relationship with this team member and that, as stated by one DMPS team member, "when this bond is in place, families are more comfortable asking questions, advocating for their child, and embedding interventions into more parts of their day." Another DMPS team member said:

> We have also learned that this service delivery approach can be fluid, with additional providers coming and going as needed based on family concerns. Sometimes families (and team members) need more support, so additional team members may be needed for longer periods of time, or sometimes for the remainder of their time in Early ACCESS. The main thing that we have learned is that it is important for all team members to be on the same page to support the family while keeping the primary liaison relationship intact.

Step by Step: Northwest AEA

Northwest AEA focused on TC2, working together as a team "to systematically and regularly exchange expertise, knowledge, and information to build team capacity and jointly solve problems, plan, and implement interventions" (DEC, 2014, p. 15). In 2012, providers stopped bringing toy bags on home visits and began engaging the family in their child's intervention during activities and routines using the family's materials. From 2012 to 2016, the Early Childhood Department in the Northwest AEA reviewed research around the shift in practice from traditional child-focused practice to coaching families. Agency leaders within the department prioritized frequent opportunities to learn about evidence-based practices on family capacity building and coaching. They developed professional learning communities, brought in speakers to Northwest AEA and conducted monthly Early Childhood Department meetings. The early childhood staff also participated in ongoing training in FGRBI through the distance mentoring model provided by Florida State University. AEA leaders decided initially that only Early ACCESS early childhood special education teachers would participate in the professional development. As these teachers implemented their new skills, they shared and presented interactive activities to promote coaching with other disciplines (i.e., PT, OT, SLPs). The ongoing, intentional focus on TC2 was a critical component of their growth.

In 2016, Northwest AEA began using a team structure with primary liaisons in their work with families (TC5). It was a natural progression for educators who were coaching with fidelity and questioning the efficiency and effectiveness of multiple team members visiting the families. They gathered data on their program, including the number of intakes, IFSPs, IEPs, and referrals. Using these data, they reduced from 14 teams to 11 teams and then reorganized into eight teams with the full support of the special education director. They completed a book study using *The Early Intervention Teaming Handbook* (Shelden & Rush, 2013) and used it to guide the teaming process. At each monthly professional development meeting, they now schedule time for reflection on what is working and what they can do to improve. The agenda always includes the vision and mission of Early ACCESS as well as a link to the DEC Recommended Practices and the Early Intervention Key Principles (Workgroup on Principles and Practices in Natural Environments, 2008) to keep them grounded.

Agency leaders attribute much of their success to the positive commitment of the team members and their continued focus on providing quality early intervention to the children and families in their region with the support of the administrators. The program director noted:

> We have challenges too, including limited access to providers such as OTs, PTs, and SLPs who also serve K–12 populations. These specialists have not been able to join our Early Childhood Department or professional development meetings consistently to study research and to reflect. We plan to use our internal coach to increase individual coaching with them using videos, reviewing the key components of FGRBI and reflection.

Right Time, Right Plan: Green Hills AEA

"We may have had the cart ahead of the horse" is one way to describe the Green Hills AEA change process. Green Hills team members began a pilot project several years ago starting with TC5. They gained important information from their pilot project. While the primary liaison approach was their goal, they did not feel

> Agency leaders attribute much of their success to the positive commitment of the team members and their continued focus on providing quality early intervention to the children and families in their region with the support of the administrators.

that the teams had the necessary knowledge, skills, and resources for implementation. An internal coach shared:

> While Green Hills AEA has not disallowed time for weekly team meetings, staff find it difficult to meet weekly to collaborate and discuss families. One potential barrier is the fact that our OT/PT staff serve birth to 21 years of age and have school caseloads. This makes it difficult at times to plan for regularly scheduled collaboration in the birth to 3 world.

They realized they had to do more than "disallow." They needed to be proactive if they were all going to get on the same page of service delivery, which was essential for the primary liaison model. They developed a compromise of two regional meetings each month in which several "mini" meetings occur simultaneously, concluding with time for professional development for everyone. An administrator noted:

> We are doing better [at] eliminating the minutia (e.g., scheduling) and leaving that to e-mail or discussion outside of our team meeting. We have come to understand that technology is our friend in teaming and utilize this often with our busy schedules and extended distances.

Early intervention team members now believe that coaching each other through tricky situations and cross training is important in supporting the family's needs. As team members' confidence has increased through their experience coaching families, they are seeing how they can coach colleagues using similar practices such as reflection and problem-solving. All team members use video to record their home visits and share with their team. Video feedback and coaching are integrated into the team meetings so all team members are included in conversations, outcome writing, and coordination. The administrator noted that "we have a plan, are collecting data, and are going to take the time for everyone to move forward together through professional development and teaming." The team's vision is that primary liaisons for each family will be a natural outcome of these efforts in the years to come.

Three Lessons Learned

Engage Leadership

Leadership and support from state and local administration were crucial for the AEAs to move forward with their shifts in service delivery and teaming and collaboration efforts. Adopting a statewide model of service delivery that includes teaming and collaboration helped to serve as an anchor across each of the AEAs, despite their varying structures. The statewide EAGL team's commitment to systems change as a process, along with the additional professional development resources, supported the changes in practice the AEAs desired or had under way. Open dialogue at the EAGL team meetings, an appreciation of differences

Early intervention team members now believe that coaching each other through tricky situations and cross training is important in supporting the family's needs.

between agencies, and recognition of the importance of measurement and high expectations facilitated the process. The EAGL team's support of the common statewide goal of implementation of FGRBI with teaming and collaboration practices embedded in it has encouraged continued effort even when challenges such as administrative changes or budget cuts occurred. The EAGL team encouraged problem-solving and reflection on what worked, under what conditions, and what was not working in order to learn from each other. Quarterly written updates documented their progress. At the AEA level, administrative support increased the rate of change and the adoption of teaming practices as illustrated by a quote from Northwest AEA:

> We learn together as a team, work together toward common goals, and use data to inform decision-making. The early childhood department supervisor now shares information and resources with the administrative cabinet meetings weekly regarding the shift to FGRBI using coaching and a primary liaison. We have shared video with the cabinet so they know what we are doing to support our youngest children and families.

Other AEAs with less direct connection to their administrators identify the importance of marketing their approach to their leadership to increase visibility, understanding of the model, resources, and support.

Make Time to Be a Team, Collaborate, and Learn Together

Although the frequency, size, and structure for team meetings varies among AEAs, the importance of team meetings was emphasized by the AEAs and the EAGL team. Early ACCESS team members across the AEAs reported that working with each other on a regular basis was important for changing practice, building trust, learning to coordinate services, and supporting the coaching process. An administrator shared that "weekly team meetings are a focused opportunity to collaborate and interact with each other about the children and families served. We can get and stay on the same page when we communicate frequently." It is key to have organization and structure to the meetings so they have a clear purpose. She added, "We do not want to spend our time scheduling or having agency memos read to us."

Time spent working with team members can build trust and collaboration. Another AEA, Grant Wood, had one field office that served a relatively large population. But because they served a smaller geographic area, team members connected regularly at the office. As a result, they were able to move forward with a primary liaison approach because they could study together, meet regularly, and share information with and about families. However, even in the same AEA, not all field offices were able to move forward at the same pace or use the same strategies. Multiple roles across special education agencies (e.g., Early ACCESS, plus Part B services as itinerant staff), multiple team meetings across large areas, and staff reassignments all interfered with consensus building and progress toward implementation with fidelity. This message was repeated frequently in the more rural areas of the state. Many regions statewide are not able to coordinate weekly team meetings because of time and personnel constraints. However, in 2019, time for teaming will be available across the AEAs. This major accomplishment was achieved by each region working with its leaders and will support further progress in implementation of the Teaming and Collaboration recommended practices.

The importance of the integration of TC1 and TC2 was discussed by the majority of the AEAs as an integral component of their change process. For team members, frequent meetings not only support coordinated services for

children and families but also provide a venue to coach each other and problem-solve on implementation of FGRBI. The goals of team meetings expanded as they worked together to discuss the implementation of FGRBI and coaching in general and to address specific family priorities, challenges, and successes. These discussions were led by the internal coaches assigned to their team. Because internal coaches are also team members, meetings can accomplish multiple purposes that improve the quality of services for children and families.

DMPS and Northwest AEA highlight the integration of TC1, TC2, and TC3 in supporting their capacity to implement TC5, the use of a primary liaison. An administrator said "it was a natural progression to use the primary liaison as providers became better at using FGRBI and coaching, but it was not without challenges." In DMPS, a teacher noted:

> We are still learning to identify the best fit for children who may have multiple needs and will potentially be in our program for up to three years. We know the needs may change and evolve over time and different providers may be needed at two months of age versus two years. We know that it is possible to support each other and the family as these needs change, but we are still learning the best way

to use the primary liaison approach to serve children who are in the program from infancy through transition.

In contrast to other AEAs, Central Rivers AEA in middle Iowa started the change process with regular team meetings to support the use of the primary liaison approach for all families. The AEA is using a primary liaison with all families and identifies its next steps as implementing FGRBI with families and embedding intervention on the families' priority outcomes in their everyday routines and activities with fidelity. They are collaborating as a team and will focus on instructional and interactional recommended practices.

Use Technology to Support Teaming

Technology played an important role in teaming and collaboration practices across the state and allowed the more rural Early ACCESS providers opportunities to communicate regularly. The Iowa Department of Education established Zoom and Google Docs as standard tools for teams to facilitate information exchange. Agendas, handouts, and resources are posted for the teams prior to meetings on their Google Drive. Resources include examples of materials used with families, examples from training activities, online resources, as well as links to the Early ACCESS procedures manual. Team members may join a home visit via Zoom to answer family questions and brainstorm ideas. Families can also use Zoom to contribute to discussions in team meetings.

Videos of families and their primary liaison implementing FGRBI practices are frequently collected at home visits and shared with other core team members to develop or revise outcomes or intervention strategies. Team members also share videos with family members to encourage their reflection and feedback on the intervention process. Videos are used to support implementation with other team members during professional development meetings. Internal coaches use Zoom to network with each other, participate in professional development with FSU, and attend regional meetings. As one provider said, "I never dreamed I would say that technology is my friend, but it has certainly changed our way of work for the better!" For a state that has far more rural than urban regions, technology has been a critical way to facilitate teaming between providers and families as well as between providers and their peers.

> Technology played an important role in teaming and collaboration practices across the state and allowed the more rural Early ACCESS providers opportunities to communicate regularly.

Conclusions

This Early ACCESS statewide review of teaming and collaboration practices demonstrates that a unified vision does not necessarily require a single path. Each AEA is demonstrating progress toward its vision of using the DEC Recommended Practices to guide its programs. The Teaming and Collaboration recommended practices serve as both important outcomes for Early ACCESS and as a process to support implementation of FGRBI, the approach that providers are implementing. The AEAs identified consistent time together as key to their success in developing relationships, building consensus, and sharing information. Support from their leadership was also identified as a critical factor supporting their use of the Teaming and Collaboration recommended practices. The addition of internal coaches to support professional development with all disciplinary team members and the extensive integration of technology have positively supported participation of more team members, each with their own expertise and background. Each AEA, with unique structures, strengths, and challenges, continues on its path to strengthening its use of the Teaming and Collaboration recommended practices, which then leads to high-quality services for families. Teaming and collaboration practices are helping Iowa early intervention providers improve their practices by building on their collective knowledge and expertise.

Note

1. In this article, we use the term *team member* to refer to early childhood special educators, speech-language pathologists, occupational therapists, physical therapists, and others who provide Part C services in home-based settings. Families are also integral to the team, but in this work, we use this term to refer to the above professionals who work with families in early intervention.

References

Division for Early Childhood. (2014). *DEC recommended practices in early intervention/early childhood special education 2014*. Retrieved from http://www.dec-sped.org/dec-recommended-practices

Kashinath, S., Woods, J., & Goldstein, H. (2006). Enhancing generalized teaching strategy use in daily routines by parents of children with autism. *Journal of Speech, Language, and Hearing Research, 49*, 466–485. doi:10.1044/1092-4388(2006/036)

Lu, H.-L. (2010). Research on peer coaching in preservice teacher education – A review of literature. *Teaching and Teacher Education, 26*, 748–753. doi:10.1016/j.tate.2009.10.015

Marturana, E., McComish, C., Woods, J., & Crais, E. (2011). Early intervention teaming and the primary service provider approach: Who does what, when, why, and how? *SIG 1 Perspectives on Language Learning and Education, 18*(2), 47–52. doi:10.1044/lle18.2.47

Shelden, M. L., & Rush, D. D. (2013). *The early intervention teaming handbook: The primary service provider approach*. Baltimore, MD: Paul H. Brookes.

Showers, B., & Joyce, B. (1996). The evolution of peer coaching. *Educational Leadership, 53*(6), 12–16.

Woods, J., Kashinath, S., & Goldstein, H. (2004). Effects of embedding caregiver-implemented teaching strategies in daily routines on children's communication outcomes. *Journal of Early Intervention, 26*, 175–193. doi:10.1177/105381510402600302

Woods, J., Romano, M., Brown, J., Windsor, K., Lakey, E., Kashinath, S. & Coston, J. (2017). *Family-guided routines based intervention: Key indicators* (2nd ed). Tallahassee: Communication and Early Childhood Research and

Practice Center, Florida State University. Retrieved from http://fgrbi.fsu.edu/handouts/approach5/KeyIndicatorsManual_2017.pdf

Workgroup on Principles and Practices in Natural Environments, OSEP TA Community of Practice: Part C Settings. (2008, March). *Seven key principles: Looks like/doesn't look like.* Retrieved from http://ectacenter.org/~pdfs/topics/families/Principles_LooksLike_DoesntLookLike3_11_08.pdf

8

All Our Children
State Supports for Local Early Intervention and Early Head Start Collaboration

Thomas Rendon
Melissa P. Schnurr
Iowa Department of Education

The division for early childhood (2014) recommended practices call for every adult who plays a role in the life of a young child who has or is at risk for a developmental delay or disability to engage in teaming and collaboration. The Teaming and Collaboration recommended practices are often viewed as informing how interventionists work within and among colleagues and with families; however, we also believe they can be brought to bear as different systems or programs work together to provide efficient, effective, and coordinated services. Though teaming is often thought to occur primarily through the development and implementation of the Individualized Family Service Plan (IFSP) as required by the Individuals With Disabilities Education Act (IDEA, 2004), the principles behind teaming and collaboration in the DEC Recommended Practices should extend to other community organizations that are supporting and offering services to families and their children.

Collaboration and teaming between early intervention (EI) and Early Head Start (EHS) is important because families connected with EHS are more likely to be identified as needing and receiving EI services (Love et al., 2002). Although most practitioners across a variety of disciplines believe communication and collaboration with other providers and specialists is important and necessary, few actually make it routine, "work together" (i.e., collaborate), and use the Teaming and Collaboration recommended practices (Bose & Hinojosa, 2008; Dinnebeil, McInterney, & Hale, 2006; Donegan, Ostrosky, & Fowler, 1996; Paradis, Belknap, O'Neill, Baggett, & Minkovitz, 2018).

Though written for practitioners working with families of young children with delays and disabilities, the practices are highly relevant to broader teaming and collaboration efforts between community partners and Part C service providers. Specifically, TC1 calls for a diversity of service providers and family members to work together with a united purpose, recognizing that no single professional can meet the needs of children or families. TC2 calls for the team to work together "systematically and regularly" to share knowledge and understanding, solve problems, and implement interventions. Even though these individuals may be working for different agencies and have a wide variety of responsibilities, only through regularly scheduled meetings can true coordination and collaboration occur. TC3 calls for using communication and group facilitation strategies "to enhance team functioning and interpersonal relationships with and among team members" (DEC, 2014, p. 15). When there are inherent differences in phi-

losophy, values, and purposes among organizations, or entire systems, the skills for implementing the Teaming and Collaboration recommended practices are needed more than ever to overcome barriers and create a climate where productive relationships can occur (Reagans & Zuckerman, 2001).

TC4 recommends team members help each other find and use community-based services and other resources to meet child and family needs. TC5 reminds us that all teaming and collaboration work must begin and end with the family and a team must support and trust an individual to serve as a primary liaison between the team and the family. We believe team members must understand that the primary liaison does not have to be someone directly supported by Part C funding.

At a practical level, such teaming across agencies is necessary to coordinate the multiple services families are using. Failure to collaborate can result in confusion of roles and purposes by both family members and service providers, a duplication of efforts, and, on occasion, contradictory functions where families are encouraged to do things in response to services that are in conflict (Johnson, 2001). The lack of collaboration can send a message to families that some services are not important, can represent a disrespectful posture toward other professionals, and can lead to an undervaluing of the unique services and skills those professionals bring to families.

Federal regulations also stress the importance of collaboration between Part C and EHS. The Head Start Program Performance Standards (Office of Head Start, 2016) call for coordination and collaboration with local agencies responsible for implementing IDEA to participate in child find efforts to identify children that may be eligible for Part C services (p. 48). Developing written agreements (p. 48), improving service delivery, participating in the development of the IFSP, sharing information, and participating in regular meetings (p. 49) are also specified. IDEA (2004) requires that the state's EI system, Early ACCESS, coordinate with EHS (among others) in general and specifically for child find, developing IFSPs, and transitions out of EI.

Current Project

The project described here incorporated four of the five Teaming and Collaboration recommended practices and resulted in the development of two tools that can assist partners from different agencies to better support and participate in cross-agency teaming (see Appendix A and Appendix B). As Iowa's EI Comprehensive System of Personnel Development consultant and its Head Start State Collaboration Office (HSSCO) coordinator, we were aware of the status of collaboration between EHS and Part C program staff in our state. In 2016, 279 children were being jointly served by EHS and the EI system in Iowa. An HSSCO needs assessment in 2016 found that about 75% of EHS grantees in Iowa characterized their relationship with Part C partners as above a midpoint between "nonexistent" and "works together consistently." A similar percentage reported that it was likely that EI would refer a family to EHS and that the EHS teacher or home visitor would be invited to participate in the IFSP meetings. Two-thirds said they were "very confident" that they would meet their required 10% enrollment of children with disabilities. In 2016, among the 15 EHS grantees in Iowa, seven were serving fewer than the required 10% with disabilities. The assumption is that when this percentage drops below 10%, barriers must be present that are excluding children with disabilities.

These data collected in informal conversations with EHS and EI professionals revealed that while there were relationships and collaboration occurring, it was not consistently happening across the state. Less than one third of the teams were meeting consistently, and in at least half of the EI regions, such meetings either never or rarely occurred. Statements revealed professionals on both sides did not understand one another's roles and how they could collaborate effectively.

Key Questions

We invited leaders and providers from all EHS grantees and EI regions in the state to talk about barriers to working together and to offer support so collaboration could become central to how work is done. Our assumption was that with increased coordination, barriers to inclusion could be identified and the effectiveness and efficiency of services for children and families receiving services from EI and EHS would improve. We began the project with two central questions: Can EHS and EI leaders and providers work together to create a basis for teaming and collaboration? What processes are necessary and helpful in promoting teaming and collaboration?

Methods

We invited all 15 EHS program coordinators and all 10 EI regional liaisons from each of the state service areas to choose providers to join them at an all-day

> Informal conversations with EHS and EI professionals revealed that while there were relationships and collaboration occurring, it was not consistently happening across the state.

meeting. The participants were organized into 11 teams of individuals from both the EHS and Part C systems, representing seven of the nine EI service areas and 11 of the 15 EHS grantees in the state. The leadership from each agency (typically the disabilities coordinator for EHS and the regional EI liaison) identified participants for their combined teams and were asked to physically come together for the first meeting (combined team size averaged six participants). Additional outreach after the first meeting created two additional teams that participated in the project, but their data are not included here.

The teams met together face to face locally and joined other teams from across the state virtually four times over a 14-month period. The professionals who participated from EHS included grantee directors, disabilities coordinators, and home visitors; EI representatives included service coordinators, early interventionists, and regional liaisons. Both agency leads met as equals and co-facilitated the meetings. At the state level, the meetings were facilitated by the HSSCO and the EI Comprehensive System of Personnel Development consultant, both housed within the state Department of Education.

To prepare groups to create a shared vision and mission, we asked them at the first meeting to individually answer and then reflect together on the following questions:

- How many children are served by both programs?
- What are the needs of those children and families?
- What services best address those needs?
- Who provides those services?

After sharing their reflections within each team, they created a shared vision and mission statement to represent the work that EHS and EI could do together (see Table 1).

Following the vision/mission activity, teams were introduced to a process mapping activity to better understand each other's roles in the IFSP process (screening/referral/enrollment, IFSP development/monitoring, service delivery, and transition). Teams were asked to work on one of four parts of the IFSP process and describe the steps to complete the process in a template that was prepared by the facilitators. For example, in screening/referral/enrollment:

1. What has to happen for a child to be screened? Who is screened? When? How?
2. What does the referral process entail?

The template included column headings such as "Action steps to complete the process," "EI will . . .," and "EHS will . . ." to address the roles of each agency within the process. Each part of the process had at least two teams randomly assigned. After completing the task as individual teams, they shared as a large group so teams who completed the template for the same process could come to consensus. Each team considered coordination of services within their entire service area, which usually involves several counties. The roles and responsibilities were written in general terms so they could be applied across the state. At the end, the teams created a list of roles/responsibilities for the four parts of the IFSP process, which ultimately informed the guidance document that was created later.

Table 1
Sample Vision and Mission Statements

Vision statements	Mission statements
Early Head Start (EHS) and early intervention (EI) are identifying children with special needs as early as possible and supporting families together as collaborating agencies.	EHS and EI will collaborate to identify children who qualify for early intervention and provide quality supports to young children and their families receiving early intervention/Early Head Start services.
All caregivers in a child's life are partnering to provide consistent support so the child and family can embrace their potential for success in life.	EHS and EI will collaborate with families to educate and empower them to advocate for and support their child's learning and development.
Families with young children have the supports needed for all to be healthy and productive.	EHS and EI will promote and support the readiness of families and children by enhancing the children's life as a whole.
Families feel more empowered to teach their children, and the children gain the skills necessary through consistent support.	EHS and EI will collaborate to identify strengths, services, supports, and resources to facilitate the growth and development of the family and child within their natural environments and daily routines.
EHS and EI jointly want every child and family to be happy, healthy, and successful!	EHS and EI will collaborate to provide resources, coaching, education, and services to children and families in the areas of nutrition, health, developmental monitoring, and education in their natural environments to enhance their lives and futures.
EHS and EI are creating positive outcomes to help children reach their full potential in the home and EHS environments and be ready to transition to their next setting.	EHS and EI will collaborate to guide families to the resources that help fit family and child needs through coaching and routine-based intervention.
All families and children will be supported to be ready for school and life.	EHS and EI will collaborate to build ongoing relationships to empower families to advocate for what is best for their child and family and to see them through the transition process.

After this initial meeting, the teams were brought together statewide three more times using the same means as the first meeting. Meanwhile, the teams continued to meet locally (using video conference as needed), on average about once a month. During these meetings they discussed jointly enrolled children, ways to increase informal contacts and joint visits, and strategies for ensuring

EHS personnel attend IFSP meetings and receive copies of IFSPs (all with parental consent).

At each of the three subsequent 90-minute meetings where teams physically met regionally and joined across the state virtually, we spent time celebrating successes and brainstorming solutions to barriers. The request for guidance from the state to support collaboration came during the second meeting. Much of the third and fourth meetings were spent reviewing the guidance document (Appendix A) and piloting the self-assessment (Appendix B) that was created as a result of the guidance.

Who was invited to these meetings, how they were facilitated, the content of the conversations, and the use of group input to develop guidance and recommendations all reflect use of the Teaming and Collaboration recommended practices. For example, ensuring cross-agency representation was inspired by TC1, and the TC2 practice of systematic and regular collaboration made us encourage the teams to set up regular meeting times. We modeled and encouraged open communication and the use of group facilitation strategies (TC3) such as establishing a common vision and written agreements to outline expectations and joint work. The recognition that EHS is a community-based service that requires its programs to identify and refer families to a wide variety of services (Office of Head Start, 2016, pp. 45–46) was a way to incorporate TC4. It would be impossible to identify a single practitioner to serve as a primary liaison (see TC5) if teams were not meeting regularly, coordinating work, and establishing sufficient levels of trust that they were confident the liaisons were addressing the needs of both agencies.

Results

The 11 teams of EHS and EI leaders and providers met together four times over a 14-month period to gain a better understanding of each other's roles with families and jointly create a shared process for teaming together and with families served by both programs. At the conclusion of the first meeting, comments collected from the teams revealed a desire for further discussion and collaboration, a renewed appreciation for the "opening of doors" and opportunities to share information and ideas, a recognition that EI and EHS are more similar than different, and a reinforcement of previously known practices that may have slipped away over time. Most groups decided to schedule additional follow-up meetings to further clarify roles and expectations, strengthen relationships, and determine better ways to involve EHS staff in IFSP meetings.

At the second meeting, teams from across the state reviewed successes during their work together over the previous six months. They also shared barriers that emerged during their work and then worked together to identify potential solutions to those barriers. For example, because the service areas between the EHS and EI programs do not align, some individuals had to be part of two teams. This impacts the time available for individual team participants. Teams suggested using electronic meetings to cut down on the amount of time each meeting takes, especially for those who participated on more than one team.

One team reported their increased collaboration led to more children leaving EI because their IFSP outcomes had been met.

After six months, teams reported improved relationships among team members, greater responsiveness and support from partners, timely communication leading to more frequent attendance by EHS staff at IFSP meetings, a schedule of recurring meetings, greater ease at getting copies of IFSPs (with parental consent), the ability to make direct contact with one another to address specific issues for jointly served children, and a more consistent practice of referring children to one another's programs. A number of teams reported that they engaged in joint home visits, which were viewed as successful. One team noted an increase in the number of EHS-enrolled children referred to EI, while another clarified that children could be served by EI in both home-based and center-based EHS programs. Yet another team said they were using the written memorandum of understanding (MOU) with greater purpose and added detail to make it more relevant to day-to-day functioning and coordination. One team reported their increased collaboration led to more children leaving EI because their IFSP outcomes had been met.

Teams also reported on a variety of barriers at the second meeting, including challenges with service coordination, child and family issues, geographic alignment, and successfully meeting and communicating on a regular basis. Service coordination issues included struggles to fully understand one another's procedures and systems, to effectively partner to help children reach their goals, to ensure adequate support for children in EHS classrooms, and to reduce the number of home visitors going into the home.

One team reported that mutual referrals continued to be low despite meeting together more often. Though this concern was true of only a few families, the providers noted that it was because the families did not fully understand the role of EI. When the EHS provider explained what EI looks like and how it may benefit the child, the reluctance was minimized.

Overall, providers reported that families appreciated the increased collaboration between EHS and EI. When asked how families were responding, both EHS and EI providers said families liked joint visits and even requested them. The joint visits facilitated follow-through on the child outcomes in between visits because the entire team was fully aware of activities that support the child's development, the families and the team were hearing the same information, families did not have to hear the same information or answer the same questions multiple times, and joint visits meant fewer appointments for families.

One provider noted that working with each other as a team was only possible because of communication, collaboration, and relationship building; each team member had a shared focus on supporting the child and family as they worked together. As a result, children in EHS who may benefit from EI services were quickly referred to EI because team members were already in contact with one another.

Although communication and regular meetings were essential, the logistics of maintaining these practices proved to be a barrier for many teams. Weather and busy schedules made holding consistent meetings difficult. As a result, even basic information, such as which children in EHS had an IFSP, was not readily known by EHS staff. Clarifying what child information was available and sharable required several back-and-forth exchanges.

During the second meeting, groups also reported about child development concerns, especially regarding behavior. Establishing consistent interventions and monitoring their effectiveness were ongoing challenges. In one case, a team reported on the linguistic and cultural challenges of serving a child from a non-English speaking home. Language barriers predictably made communication with families harder, and sometimes both EHS and EI staff were not

sufficiently trained to identify and address speech and language delays or disorders when they occurred with dual language learning children and families. Time was provided during this meeting for groups to meet and identify potential solutions to these barriers as a team.

At the third meeting, teams reviewed and celebrated what had been accomplished through a year's worth of teaming and collaboration. They also provided feedback on a draft guidance document that outlined recommended roles for Part C providers and community partners based on the Teaming and Collaboration recommended practices. The ideas for the guidance document were taken directly from the work identified by the teams in the process mapping activity described above and in subsequent conversations about substantive outcomes from their collaborative work.

At this point in the project, it was decided that the recommended roles should apply to any community partner, not just EHS. A final guidance document was drafted based on the feedback from the group as well as a vetting process that included a review by Head Start and EHS disabilities coordinators in the state and the state's Part C leadership group. Based on the feedback, a final draft was distributed to EHS and EI leadership. A copy of the guidance document is found in Appendix A.

At the fourth meeting in January 2018, the teams used a draft self-assessment tool that was developed based on the guidance to determine how far they had progressed in establishing clear norms and practices that supported the development of strong, collaborative working relationships and what additional work might be needed. The teams also created a short-term (six months) and long-term (one year) action plan to ensure they were implementing as many of the suggested roles and responsibilities as possible. A meeting was held in May 2018 to share plan updates, successes, and additional barriers from teams.

The clearest results of the year and a half of promoting collaboration and teaming between EI and EHS were the two documents that all teams contributed to, reviewed, and provided feedback on and used as part of their ongoing work. The guidance document (Appendix A) and the self-assessment (Appendix B) represent "wisdom from the field" as well as validation that the teaming and collaboration required by state and federal regulations and the DEC Recommended Practices improve the coordination of services.

Discussion

Infants and toddlers with developmental delays or disabilities require multiple adults in their lives to care for and support them. The more these adults communicate, build a positive relationship, and work in concert to provide a single approach to address the needs of children and their families, the better the results for the child and the family. Based on reports from the providers on teams from across the state, families appreciated the increased collaboration because it increased efficiency in communication (less duplication of information), increased the speed of referral to EI from EHS, and reduced the number of appointments for the family. In addition, providers noted that there seemed to be more follow-through of interventions when collaboration between EI and EHS was strong.

The connection of teams and the coordination of services are essential to manage the interventions by multiple adults in the life of the family and child. An intentional focus on teaming and collaboration made it possible for teams to create new norms and commitments that assure these functions are occurring. Regardless of their previous level of collaboration, all of the teams reported examples of improved functioning from better interpersonal relationships to establishing new procedures for joint home visits.

Overall, the guidance (see Appendix A) incorporates four of the five Teaming and Collaboration recommended practices. It suggests that teams should have regular team meetings (TC2) to build relationships (TC3), share information (TC1, TC2, TC4), celebrate successes, and identify joint problems. The guidance recommends creating written agreements and adding collaborative practices discussed here into an organization's policies and practices. Formalizing the procedures makes it more likely that the necessary steps to collaborating across agencies will be carried out by all parties and ensures that collaboration and teaming becomes a durable part of EHS and EI services.

Our experience shows that, provided a modicum of structure and opportunity, teams are able to collaborate and provide effective and efficient services for families and young children. A clear benefit of working with EHS means that families, especially those of low income, are more likely to be connected to Part C services (Love et al., 2002). Beginning with a clear, mutual understanding of purpose and constraints (as laid out by regulation and funders) provided

> The connection of teams and the coordination of services are essential to manage the interventions by multiple adults in the life of the family and child.

a foundation on which practitioners from the EHS and EI systems could gain appreciation, understanding, and mutual respect. Regular and systematic meetings led the teams to develop trusting relationships, a prerequisite for effective collaboration.

Establishing expectations for groups to document their work together and reflect on successes and barriers encouraged collaboration and provided a rich array of evidence of past work and planning for future work. And because the self-assessment encourages formal and informal written agreements, teams began to pay more attention to MOUs. These agreements were previously seen to be inadequate or outdated and not a necessary support for collaborative work. When the MOUs were used as part of teaming and collaboration, though, team members wanted to make sure the agreements adequately and accurately reflected and supported their mutual work. As a consequence, action plans included revising and renegotiating MOUs.

At a state level, it became apparent that EI service providers should not just be working with EHS but a wider array of community partners. Child care providers, home visitors, foster care workers, itinerant health workers, and social workers are important partners that can assist families in better using EI services as well as support families in meeting family and child IFSP outcomes. Indeed, Weglarz-Ward (2016) found that even though child care providers often served young children with disabilities and early interventionists supported them, actual collaborative activities were uncommon. The guidance developed reflects this new awareness by referring to a more generic category of providers termed *community partners.*

Conclusion

The project described here between EHS and Part C services shows that leaders and providers from both programs have a desire to work more closely together; however, they may need encouragement and opportunity to reach their full potential. Our effort involved no additional expenditures or costs, except for additional time to attend meetings that was absorbed as part of regularly assigned duties and during contracted time. While we did not have formal administrative buy-in, we ran into no administrative hurdles. Other states attempting to replicate these efforts may want to have conversations with administrators to address any concerns proactively.

In general, most agencies saw the effort as one with obvious benefits in terms of quality and efficiency as well as a clear way to fulfill regulatory requirements. State leaders from both Part C and Head Start Collaboration Offices, or other state officials who oversee early childhood services, can make an important difference by (1) promoting cross-agency teaming and collaboration that is based on the Teaming and Collaboration recommended practices and begins with a common vision, (2) focusing on specific actions that are embedded in the work of early interventionists, (3) encouraging a collaborative approach to address the needs of children with disabilities and their families, and (4) connecting with preparation programs to ensure that the "soft skills" and competencies related to teaming and collaboration are emphasized in coursework.

> Establishing expectations for groups to document their work together and to reflect on successes and barriers encouraged collaboration and provided a rich array of evidence of past work and planning for future work.

References

Bose, P., & Hinojosa, J. (2008). Reported experiences from occupational therapists interacting with teachers in inclusive early childhood classrooms. *American Journal of Occupational Therapy, 62,* 289–297. doi:10.5014/ajot.62.3.289

Dinnebeil, L. A., McInerney, W., & Hale, L. (2006). Understanding the roles and responsibilities of itinerant ECSE teachers through Delphi research. *Topics in Early Childhood Special Education, 26,* 153–166. doi:10.1177/0271121406 0260030301

Division for Early Childhood. (2014). *DEC recommended practices in early intervention/early childhood special education 2014.* Retrieved from http://www.dec-sped.org/dec-recommended-practices

Donegan, M. M., Ostrosky, M. M., & Fowler, S. A. (1996). Children enrolled in multiple programs: Characteristics, supports, and barriers to teacher communication. *Journal of Early Intervention, 20,* 95–106. doi:10.1177/105381519602000201

Iowa Family Support Network. (n.d.). What to expect. Retrieved from https://www.iafamilysupportnetwork.org/early-access-iowa/parents-family/what-to-expect-1

Johnson, K. A. (2001, May). *No place like home: State home visiting policies and programs* (Pub. No. 452). New York, NY: The Commonwealth Fund.

Love, J. M., Kisker, E. E., Ross, C. M., Schochet, P. Z., Brooks-Gunn, J., Paulsell, D., . . . Brady-Smith, C. (2002, June). *Making a difference in the lives of infants and toddlers and their families: The impacts of Early Head Start* (Vol. 1: Final Technical Report). Princeton, NJ: Mathematica Policy Research.

Office of Head Start. (2016, December 30). *Head Start program performance standards.* Washington, DC: Author. Retrieved from https://eclkc.ohs.acf.hhs.gov/sites/default/files/pdf/hspps-appendix.pdf

Paradis, H. A., Belknap, A., O'Neill, K. M. G., Baggett, S., & Minkovitz, C. S. (2018). Coordination of early childhood home visiting and health care providers. *Children and Youth Services Review, 85,* 202–210. doi:10.1016/j.childyouth.2017.12.029

Reagans, R., & Zuckerman, E. W. (2001). Networks, diversity, and productivity: The social capital of corporate R&D teams. *Organization Science, 12,* 502–517. doi:10.1287/orsc.12.4.502.10637

Weglarz-Ward, J. M. (2016). *Project Collaborative Care: Experiences of child care and early intervention providers* (Doctoral dissertation). Available from ProQuest Dissertations and Theses database. (UMI No. 10609940)

Appendix A
Guidance for Collaboration Between Community Partners and Early ACCESS

The DEC Recommended Practices call on all professionals who work with young children and their families to engage in "teaming and collaboration practices that promote and sustain collaborative adult partnerships, relationships, and ongoing interactions to ensure that programs and services achieve desired child and family outcomes and goals" (DEC, 2014, p. 15). This guidance is designed to promote coordination and collaboration among Early ACCESS providers and their community partners (e.g., Early Head Start, child care including family child care, home visitation programs, child welfare agency) by clarifying roles and responsibilities so appropriate expectations are understood, opportunities for connections are increased, and service duplication and gaps are addressed (see Appendix B).

The ultimate goal is to increase the effectiveness and efficiency of services for children and families receiving services from Early ACCESS and additional programs. As with everything in the IFSP process, partnership with community organizations should be done through engagement with parents and caregivers, including the consent to exchange information about the child and family.

What follows is general guidance for Early ACCESS providers and their community partners who have children receiving Early ACCESS services or have children potentially eligible for Early ACCESS services. The guidance is organized around four key phases in the provision of Early ACCESS services:

1. Screening, referral and enrollment
2. IFSP development
3. Service delivery (IFSP implementation/monitoring)
4. Transition

Screening/Referral/Enrollment	
Early ACCESS	**Community Partner**
1. Understand the purpose of community partner programs and enough information about what the programming entails to inform families if a referral is needed.	1. Understand the purpose of Early ACCESS and enough information about what services entail to inform families if a referral is needed. (See Iowa Family Support Network, n.d.; Workgroup on Principles and Practices in Natural Environments, 2018)
2. Identify and form relationships with community partners (beyond medical providers) in your service area who are doing routine screening for developmental, behavioral, and sensory delays or concerns. These partners serve as referral sources.	2. If your agency is doing routine screening for developmental, behavioral, and sensory delays or concerns, inform local Early ACCESS providers so they are aware and understand your procedures for sharing results. Refer families to Early ACCESS as necessary.
3. Use screening data provided by community partners as much as possible and support them to make improvements in their screening procedures when needed. Cooperate with community partners if additional data collection is needed.	3. Inform the family of the screening results and get their permission to make the referral to Early ACCESS. Provide all evidence you have collected when families are referred and make sure you have parental permission to share data in advance. Cooperate with Early ACCESS if additional data collection is needed.

Appendix A (continued)
Guidance for Collaboration Between Community Partners and Early ACCESS

Screening/Referral/Enrollment (continued)

Early ACCESS	Community Partner
4. On an annual basis, develop written agreements with community partners that describe the data needed to make an eligibility determination so community partners can help identify and determine potentially eligible children.	4. Work with Early ACCESS to develop written agreements that include what data you are willing to provide and how that data can be shared with Early ACCESS. If possible, make needed adjustments to your screening procedures and tools to facilitate the identification and eligibility of children.

IFSP Development

Early ACCESS	Community Partner
1. Include any adult directly and regularly interacting with the child (i.e., involved with daily routines and activities) in the development of the IFSP (outcomes, strategies, etc.). Identifying and involving those adults should be done with full knowledge and consent of parents and other caregivers. If not able to attend physically, the service coordinator should gather relevant information from these adults.	1. When a child in your program is enrolled in Early ACCESS, communicate with the Early ACCESS service coordinator about how the representatives from your program can be involved in the IFSP development, taking into consideration the desires of parents or other caregivers. Make an effort to participate actively in the IFSP team as possible and needed. Involvement should include sharing relevant information about the child and family based on your ongoing involvement with them. Ensure the IFSP team understands what services you are providing to the family and child.
2. As part of the IFSP development process (not necessarily as part of the IFSP itself) and using a collaborative process, establish clear and mutually agreed upon roles, procedures, and strategies for Early ACCESS early interventionists, caregivers, and community partners to perform as part of the IFSP implementation. The goal is a single plan for implementation that describes what is done and who does it so all work related to the IFSP is coordinated and not duplicative of other services.	2. Participate in a collaborative process with Early ACCESS to establish all roles, procedures, and strategies related to the IFSP outcomes and meeting those outcomes. Know what supports are needed to perform those roles, follow procedures, or implement the strategies. Ensure that the IFSP team understands how the roles, procedures, and strategies support your family/child plan. These issues should be addressed and resolved as part of the IFSP development process.

Appendix A (continued)
Guidance for Collaboration Between Community Partners and Early ACCESS

Service Delivery (IFSP Implementation/Monitoring)	
Early ACCESS	**Community Partner**
1. Equip and support community partners and other caregivers to perform the desired, coordinated work. Participate in trainings and meetings offered by community partners as necessary to perform the coordinated work. Create and use mutually agreed-upon check-in process to evaluate roles, procedures, and strategy implementation to support IFSP team members and community partners. Monitor child and family progress and use the information to continuously improve the processes.	1. Participate in trainings and meetings as necessary to perform the coordinated work. Create and use mutually agreed-upon check-in process to evaluate roles, procedures, and strategy implementation to support IFSP team members and community partners. Monitor child and family progress and use the information to continuously improve the processes.
2. Establish at least monthly communication with community partners to share progress monitoring data, make adjustments in implementation plans, and coordinate activities as needed. It is both parties' responsibility to make sure communication occurs and communication is, by definition, two-way (maybe multilateral if more than two partners involved.) All parties need to be willing to share data relevant to the child's IFSP outcomes, current status, and progress toward reaching those outcomes. If transfer of protected information is involved, consent from families to share information among partners and Early ACCESS is required.	2. Establish at least monthly communication with the Early ACCESS service coordinator to share progress monitoring data, make adjustments in implementation plans, and coordinate activities as needed. It is both parties' responsibility to make sure communication occurs and communication is, by definition, two-way (maybe multilateral if more than two partners involved.) All parties need to be willing to share data relevant to the child's IFSP outcomes, current status, and progress toward reaching those outcomes. If transfer of protected information is involved, consent from families to share information among partners and Early ACCESS is required.
3. Establish in writing how communication between Early ACCESS and community partners is initiated and reciprocated and how disputes among parties are resolved.	3. Establish in writing how communication between Early ACCESS and community partners is initiated and reciprocated and how disputes among parties are resolved.

Appendix A (continued)
Guidance for Collaboration Between Community Partners and Early ACCESS

Transition

Early ACCESS	Community Partner
1. Provide families options for services once the child turns 3, including early childhood special education (Part B) services, if needed, and support the family in choosing their next steps.	1. Help to ensure families are aware of service options once the child turns 3.
2. Identify the needed supports for all children (regardless of whether they will continue with Part B or not) to best support them during their transition to their new setting.	2. Understand the needed supports for all children after they turn 3 and offer to provide those supports if appropriate and if the community partner is able to.
3. Communicate with the new service providers, share data after receiving parent consent, and provide necessary information regarding supports for the child to be successful in the new setting. Understand what supports and services are available in the new setting/program. Work with partner to prepare the best possible environment to support success.	3. Gather family and child information from Early ACCESS service coordinator and share any additional information partner program has so there is a joint understanding of what will support the child to be successful in the new setting/program. Work with Early ACCESS to prepare the best possible environment to support success.
4. Provide support for the family, the child, and the community partner to be prepared for the transition to the new setting, including equipping parents to be advocates for their child. Work with family, child, and community partners to help family understand the new setting/program through written materials, conversations, and visits when possible. Include policies, procedures, and opportunities for family engagement in the new setting. Support child's transition to new setting/program through activities such as visits, talking about changes, sharing photos or items between home and the program, and sharing routines from home and those of the new program.	4. Provide support for the family and the child to be prepared for the transition to the new setting, including equipping parents to be advocates for their child. Work with family, child, and Early ACCESS to help family understand the new setting/program through written materials, conversations, and visits when possible. Include policies, procedures, and opportunities for family engagement in the new setting. Support child's transition to new setting/program through activities such as visits, talking about changes, sharing photos or items between home and the program, and sharing routines from home and those of the new program.

Appendix B
Self-Assessment for Collaboration Between Community Partners and Early ACCESS

This self-assessment is intended for use by both Early ACCESS and its community partners, ideally as a team together. Use this document to gauge how well teams are collaborating and make plans for improvement moving forward. Use this document alongside Appendix A.

Team member names: _____

Date of assessment completion: _____

Screening/Referral/Enrollment	Doing	Partially Doing	Not Doing
1. Understand the purpose of the programs available to infants, toddlers, and their families in your area and have enough information about what the programming entails to inform families if a referral is needed.			
2. Be aware of all programs and providers in your area doing routine screening of infants and toddlers for developmental, behavioral, and sensory delays.			
3. Have in place a procedure for sharing screening data among partners, with the family's permission.			
4. Develop and use written agreements among partners that describe the process for sharing screening data and any other data useful in making eligibility decisions for Early ACCESS.			
NOTES:			

IFSP Development	Doing	Partially Doing	Not Doing
1. All adults that directly and regularly interact with the child are involved with IFSP development, with the family's permission. Involvement may include presence at the IFSP meetings or invited input and information at the meeting via the Early ACCESS service coordinator.			
2. Establish clear and mutually agreed-upon roles, procedures, and strategies for all involved with the child/family so that all work related to the IFSP is coordinated and not duplicative of other services.			
NOTES:			

Appendix B (continued)
Self-Assessment for Collaboration Between Community Partners and Early ACCESS

Service Delivery (IFSP implementation/monitoring)	Doing	Partially Doing	Not Doing
1. Participate in trainings and meetings as necessary to perform the coordinated work.			
2. Create and use mutually agreed-upon check-in process to evaluate roles, procedures, and strategy implementation to support all providers involved with the child/family.			
3. Coordinate the collection of information on a child's and family's progress.			
4. Communicate monthly with all partners with shared children/families to share data on their progress, make adjustments in implementation plans, and coordinate activities as needed. If transfer of protected information is involved, obtain consent from families to share information among partners and Early ACCESS.			
5. Use a written plan that outlines how communication between Early ACCESS and community partners is initiated and reciprocated.			
6. Write agreements with partners that include dispute resolution procedures.			
NOTES:			

Appendix B (continued)
Self-Assessment for Collaboration Between Community Partners and Early ACCESS

Transition	Doing	Partially Doing	Not Doing
1. Ensure families are aware of service options before the child turns 3.			
2. Identify how to best support children during their transition from Early ACCESS to new service options.			
3. Work with partners who have been involved with the child/family up to age 3 to prepare the best possible environment to support success.			
4. Prepare the family, the child, and all partners for the transition to the new setting, including equipping parents to be advocates for their child.			
5. Work with family, child, and all partners to help family understand the new setting/program through written materials, conversations, and visits when possible.			
6. Share with families the policies, procedures, and opportunities for their engagement in the new setting.			
7. Support child's transition to new setting/program through activities such as visits, talking about changes, sharing photos or items between home and the program, and sharing routines from home and those of the new program.			
NOTES:			

9

Technical Assistance and Professional Learning for Teaming and High-Quality Inclusion

EMILY ROPARS
ANN KREMER
Early CHOICES

M AXIMIZING RESOURCES TO PROVIDE PROFESSIONAL LEARN-ing that is high quality and moves an early childhood program to sustained implementation of a practice is a challenge Early CHOICES has been grappling with since 2014. Early CHOICES, a small state-funded project in Illinois, provides training and technical assistance to increase the number of preschoolers who have access to high-quality inclusive environments. To maximize our efforts, we use a team-based model to build on the collective knowledge of the classroom teams. The strategy helps build teaming and collaboration across the program and increases the quality of inclusive practices within the classrooms. This article describes how a collaboration between Early CHOICES and an early childhood program resulted in a yearlong professional learning series that used a team-based model for change (Bailey, McWilliam, & Winton, 1992; Winton, McWilliam, Harrison, Owens, & Bailey, 1992), integrated the program's continuous quality improvement cycle related to inclusion, and supported teaming and collaboration. The authors are the project director and full-time LRE specialist for Early CHOICES, who bring many years of collective experience supporting inclusive practices as teachers, administrators, and technical assistance providers.

Inclusion in Illinois

Inclusion has a long history in Illinois, starting in 1988 with a federal grant that focused on inclusion of students with disabilities from ages 3 to 21 called Project CHOICES (Children Have Opportunities in Inclusive Classrooms, Environments, and Schools). In July 2014, Early CHOICES became a stand-alone project outside of the school-age (6–21) training and technical assistance projects operated through a grant awarded by the Illinois State Board of Education (ISBE) to the School Association for Special Education in DuPage County using IDEA discretionary funds. Early CHOICES assists ISBE in meeting local needs by providing services throughout Illinois. The project staff is small; three full-time staff serve all 750 local education agencies that serve children ages 3–5. To maximize our capacity, we partner with other technical assistance projects serving the Illinois early childhood community, including the Illinois Support and Technical Assistance Regional Network (STARNET), Illinois Early Childhood Professional Learning, and the Early Intervention Training Program at the University of Illinois.

Early CHOICES supports inclusive practices across Illinois by targeting its work in three areas aligned with the DEC/NAEYC (2009) joint position statement on inclusion:

1. Providing technical assistance regarding organizational change at the systems level with programs to improve access for children with disabilities to learning environments with typically developing peers.
2. Supporting programs that have increased access for children with disabilities to inclusive classrooms to begin the initial implementation of high-quality inclusive practices.
3. Engaging with targeted programs through professional learning to examine their practices used in inclusive classrooms to assure the high-quality practices are reaching all children with disabilities.

Our focus in this article is on our professional learning responsibilities. Early CHOICES uses implementation science as a foundation for its work. When Illinois received technical assistance from the State Implementation and Scaling-up of Evidence-based Practices Center (n.d.) from 2008–2010, the Early CHOICES project director was a member of the Illinois state leadership team. The three implementation drivers identified by Fixsen and colleagues—professional competency, leadership, and organization drivers—influence how we plan our training and technical assistance with programs to assure each program is building toward full implementation of evidence-based practices (Fixen, Naoom, Blase, Friedman, & Wallace, 2005).

More recently, Illinois used Race to the Top Early Learning Challenge (RTT-ELC) funds to build the Quality Rating and Improvement System (QRIS) system, which included an Award of Excellence for Inclusion as part of the state program rating system. Early CHOICES worked closely in the development of the award and received additional funds to support programs in applying for it. Early CHOICES provided training to staff to use the Inclusive Classroom Profile (ICP) as a self-reflection tool to identify the professional learning needs and strengths of programs applying for the award of excellence. The ICP is a structured, reliable, and valid observation assessment tool designed to assess the quality of daily inclusive classroom practices that support the developmental needs of children with disabilities in early childhood settings (Soukakou, 2012; Soukakou, Winton, West, Sideris, & Rucker, 2014). The ICP is organized into 12 items that indicate high-quality inclusion: adaptations of space, materials, and equipment; adult

involvement in peer interactions; adults' guidance of children's free-choice activities and play; conflict resolution; membership; relationships between adults and children; support for communication; adaptations of group activities; transitions between activities; feedback; family-professional partnerships; and monitoring children's learning. In 2015, Early CHOICES provided funding for its staff to be trained to reliability on the ICP by certified reliability trainers from the Frank Porter Graham Child Development Institute at the University of North Carolina at Chapel Hill. We continue to use the ICP as a tool for two purposes: developing program staff's understanding of the practices that support children with disabilities in inclusive settings and self-reflection and goal setting related to their practices.

Early CHOICES and Professional Learning

Early CHOICES evaluates its efforts annually to be sure that its work aligns with both the literature regarding effective professional learning, which includes modeling, feedback, and ongoing coaching (Joyce & Showers, 2002; Snyder, Hemmeter, & McLaughlin, 2011), and the DEC Recommended Practices regarding inclusion of children with disabilities (Division for Early Childhood [DEC], 2014). In reviewing the literature on effective professional learning, we saw a "disconnect" between the research and our practices. Early CHOICES had been offering workshops that provided a one-day opportunity for individuals to participate as teams, but in practice, most often individuals attended as single representatives of their programs. We often offered site-based professional learning; however, we wanted to increase our job-embedded professional learning with an emphasis on consultation, coaching, and facilitated collaboration among staff in all roles of the program, as defined in the literature on effective professional development (National Professional Development Center on Inclusion, 2008).

Early CHOICES used the DEC Recommended Practices as the source of evidence on effective inclusion practices. Based on our use of a team-based model of change, where teams participate in planning for, reflecting on, and implementing new practices or programs, we particularly highlighted the Teaming and Collaboration recommended practices. We know the benefits of collaboration do not just impact adults; enhancing collaboration among staff in schools has been shown to have positive outcomes for students (Joyce & Calhoun, 2010). Therefore, Early CHOICES wanted to develop professional learning using a team-based model of change, strengthening teaming and collaboration, using the ICP as the tool to build a shared understanding of the practices that support children in inclusive settings.

Pilot Site

The Ann Reid Early Childhood Center (ARECC) in Naperville, Illinois, approached Early CHOICES about a partnership to examine its inclusive practices, and this became the perfect opportunity to implement the professional learning series with a program. At the start of our partnership, ARECC served 469 preschool-age children, which included 157 children who qualified for the at-risk program and 135 typically developing children whose families paid tuition. Most of the 138 children with disabilities were included in the regular early childhood program, with only five being served in a separate setting. The program is richly diverse in culture and languages. As of April 2018, 170 children qualified for English language learner services, and children and their families spoke 34 languages. Students with Individual Education Programs (IEPs) at the early childhood level are educated alongside typically developing peers

Courtesy of Frank Porter
Graham Child Development
Institute

and receive the majority of their supports and services within that setting. The classroom teachers have early childhood education certification as well as endorsements in special education and English as a second language. The program has a QRIS rating of Gold, which is the highest level of quality in Illinois. In addition, the program received an award of excellence in cultural and linguistic practices, also through QRIS.

In recent years, ARECC has reduced the number of separate settings for children with disabilities, and in 2018 it had only one noninclusive classroom. The program model changed because of its commitment to inclusion as well as the districtwide goal of increasing inclusive environments for students. The program's leadership team, composed of the principal, assistant principal, and instructional leader, sought to inform and strengthen the program's inclusive practices as they adapted its program model. Because the program had participated in the award of excellence in another focus area, the leadership team had experience in bringing staff together for an intensive, programwide inquiry (i.e., organizing staff into work groups and allocating appropriate time for team meetings). The program was already implementing high-quality, developmentally appropriate practices and had many structures in place to support teaming and collaboration, such as professional learning communities, shared planning time, and data-based decision making. These strengths of the program allowed for the collaboration to focus on capacity building around inclusion because some of the foundational aspects for using a team-based model of change were already in place.

Early CHOICES encourages programs to implement strategies that intentionally engage all stakeholders from the beginning, particularly around their vision for inclusion in their program to build team capacity and jointly solve issues related to their vision (TC2). ARECC's leadership team recognized that although most of the program had been inclusive, by reducing self-contained classrooms to one section some staff were being asked to adjust their roles to support children in inclusive classrooms rather than serving them in a separate setting. We agreed that to move forward, the program would review the vision statement to assure a shared understanding with all staff. To support active engagement, the series was designed to provide multiple opportunities for staff to participate in discussions and planning sessions with colleagues within their classroom team and beyond (TC2, TC3). For programs to support interdisciplinary teaming and for program staff to collaborate to meet the needs of children and families, all staff needed to be present during the professional learning and meetings (TC1, TC2). For this professional learning series, all 80 professionals working in the program, including teachers, paraeducators, related service staff, the program's leadership team, and the diagnostic team, were present and participated in all of the activities. In many programs, paraeducators are not provided with the same professional learning opportunities as other staff because of their contracts and/or work hours. It is significant that ARECC supports paraeducators by encouraging their growth through a professional learning community and by having them attend all dates of the series in this collaborative professional learning opportunity (TC1, TC2).

Developing a Professional Learning Series

In the process of organizational change, such as in this instance of moving toward improved inclusive opportunities and classroom practices, it is important to examine staff members' perception of the program's readiness for change and how the program could change (Eby, Adams, Russell, & Gaby, 2000). Attitudes and beliefs are often the greatest challenge to inclusion, and more specifically, a lack of communication and collaboration can be a barrier (Barton & Smith, 2015). The program leadership team and Early CHOICES took both recommended best practices for professional learning as well as the importance of attitudes and beliefs into consideration when developing the content of the series. They agreed on a professional learning series that included foundational information

> Based on our use of a team-based model of change, where teams participate in planning for, reflecting on, and implementing new practices or programs, we particularly highlighted the Teaming and Collaboration recommended practices.

regarding inclusion, a study of the Inclusive Classroom Profile, opportunities to engage in facilitated discussions with their teams, observations in their classrooms, and action planning related to their observations. The series consisted of four days spread across the 2017–2018 school year, with dates in August, September, October, and March. To create a professional learning experience that is interactive and meaningful, Early CHOICES intentionally planned for different groupings of staff, posed guiding questions for discussion, and provided multiple modalities for reflection, including group debrief, individual reflection time, and small/large group discussions (TC1, TC2).

Day one consisted of an overview of inclusion research facts, data, and legal foundations drawn from the federal policy position statement on preschool inclusion (U.S. Department of Health and Human Services & U.S. Department of Education, 2015). Following an overview of the selected research facts, Early CHOICES provided guiding questions to facilitate and enhance conversations among classroom teams: What are you curious about? Does the foundational information confirm your knowledge about and/or experiences with inclusion? (TC2). To further support an understanding of inclusion at the program and classroom levels, Early CHOICES presented the "What Makes Inclusion Work?" planning tool and infographic (Early CHOICES, n.d.-c). The planning tool highlights eight aspects of early childhood programming that support inclusion: vision and attitude, professional learning, formal time to plan and reflect, administrative support, family and community partnerships, adaptations and support systems, evidence-based practices, and collaboration and teaming. Early CHOICES facilitated staff dialogue by giving reflective feedback and providing guiding questions to support the classroom teams in discussing strengths and opportunities for growth related to inclusion. These conversations provided an opportunity for those more experienced with inclusion to reflect on the program and those with less experience to learn more about inclusionary practices (TC3). Early CHOICES facilitated a debriefing in which teams could share their group's priorities for future learning (TC2).

The second day in the series specifically explored the ICP. To provide a context for the day, Early CHOICES reviewed the defining features of inclusion (DEC/NAEYC, 2009): access, participation, and supports. Participants were encouraged to look for those features in the indicators of the ICP. To build upon the program's collective knowledge and experiences, Early CHOICES asked the staff to take a sticky note and write down what they consider to be a feature of high-quality inclusion. They were then asked to go stand by the poster most closely related to their feature of quality (access, participation, or support). After Early CHOICES defined each indicator, a representative from each group read some highlights of what their colleagues wrote, reinforcing the learning and providing an opportunity for the staff to be confident in the knowledge they had to use as a foundation for inclusion (TC2, TC3).

Supporting Teaming and Collaboration With the ICP

To learn about the ICP, the group had multiple opportunities to engage with the 12 items. The ICP defines each of the items with indicators on a rubric

> These conversations provided an opportunity for those more experienced with inclusion to reflect on the program and those with less experience to learn more about inclusionary practices.

(1-inadequate, 3-minimal, 5-good, 7-excellent). Early CHOICES knows that programs need to see practices in action to develop an understanding of what they look like and how they might be used within their program. To support this within the context of Illinois, we filmed and developed a collection of videos (Early CHOICES, n.d.-a) featuring programs that had achieved the Award of Excellence for Inclusion. These videos highlight high-quality inclusive classrooms and are aligned with specific items on the ICP. To continue the interdisciplinary collaboration as well as to support staff in building team capacity, the staff worked together in several configurations to explore the material, first as classroom teams, then by discipline, then randomly (TC1, TC2). The participants were given conversation prompts to encourage engagement with each other. For example, after hearing about the first two items on the ICP, the group divided by role to discuss how their role supports these practices and what might be some aspects for future team inquiry (TC1, TC2, TC3). To make participation from all staff more likely, the groups were asked to respond in a "round robin" style, with each participant having a turn to voice his or her opinion as they went around their circle (TC3). The small groups then reported back to the larger group. The program leadership team and Early CHOICES used this information to develop the next date in the professional learning series.

At first glance, the ICP items seem "obvious" to practitioners who feel they have them in place. So, it is important that professionals discuss them and the corresponding indicators as a team to notice the nuances and the individualization of supports in the highest levels on the rubric (TC2, TC3). To support this dialogue, Early CHOICES (2017) provided a reflection tool it developed as a companion to the ICP workbook and manual. The tool has space to take notes and to document priorities for future learning related to the ICP. Early CHOICES wanted to direct participants' attention to the details in the indicators at the higher end of the ICP rubric because focusing those details can often reveal some gaps in practices. For example, after learning about "Adults' Guidance of Children's Free-Choice Activities and Play," classroom teams were prompted to discuss the following questions: How do we collect data regarding individual child interventions? How do we dedicate planning time to collaborate around data interpretation and share that information with families? (TC1, TC2, TC3, TC5)

At the conclusion, the staff developed a plan to observe in their classrooms. Early CHOICES strongly encourages programs to provide an opportunity for staff in all roles to observe because it contributes multiple perspectives of the classrooms' strengths and areas for growth. Additionally, the subsequent discussion provides an opportunity for professional discourse among staff who typically do not have a chance to engage with their colleagues in this manner (TC2). The administration supported each classroom team by providing a substitute teacher for part of a day. Staff were prompted to be sure they observed the following for each item: occurrence, frequency, context, consistency, and individualization.

Before the third day of the series, staff observed their own classrooms, using the reflection tool as a guide. Individual classroom teams met during their weekly team meeting to share observations and reach a consensus on where their practices fall on the ICP rubric. The process required all staff to discuss strengths in their classrooms and identify opportunities to support the individual needs of the children in their classroom more intentionally (TC1, TC2, TC3). When Early CHOICES surveyed the staff electronically after the ICP observations, staff reported the benefits from observing and collaborating. As one teacher reported, "We used the ICP to look at different aspects of our classroom" and using the ICP helped by "making goals more accessible to everyone on the team." Responses from paraeducators also confirmed that the observation and debriefing had a positive impact on their participation in teaming. They reported "better communications between team and families," "better classroom collaboration," and "more confidence when dealing with [a] difficult situation." The feedback

illustrates how observation and debriefing can provide an opportunity for teams to engage with one another about their classroom practices (TC2).

Early CHOICES facilitated the third date in the series to allow teams to debrief regarding the observation and consensus process and to look at the nuances of the ICP indicators. ARECC has 16 classrooms. To structure their professional learning communities, the program divides the program into four pods composed of four classroom teams. Early CHOICES used this existing structure to organize the interactive pieces of this date. To encourage engagement and collaboration among classroom teams and multiteam pods, the day had three opportunities for teaming within different groups (TC1, TC2, TC3). First, to support ongoing programwide discussions, the teams reported back to each other and discussed how they came to a consensus regarding the practices following their observations (TC2, TC3). They then spent time as classroom teams using an action plan developed by Early CHOICES (n.d.-b) to embed more opportunities for the practices from the ICP within daily routines, based on the child's interests (TC1, TC2, TC3; Bricker, Pretti-Frontczak, & McComas, 1998). Second, classroom teams merged with other teams in their pods to discuss the top three practices they decided to focus on in their classrooms as well as the goals they developed (improving/expanding context, consistency, or individualization), and they then documented those goals on a poster board (TC1).

Finally, the participants did a museum walk to learn from each other (TC2). At the end of the day, we asked for feedback and reflections from the day. A few common themes emerged. First, staff said they had expertise in some of the areas they had identified as learning goals, but they did not have an opportunity to share it with colleagues in a formal way. Rather, the staff only briefly shared the goals in team meetings or when opportunities for modeling occurred incidentally in the classroom. Another common theme from staff was a need to communicate more frequently regarding specific strategies and techniques used by related service staff to support children in their classrooms.

Early CHOICES facilitated a planning call with the program leadership to debrief and use information gathered from staff to inform the fourth and final day (TC2). To provide an opportunity for collaboration across disciplines and classrooms on the final day of the series, we decided to use "coffee talks" in which program staff could focus on priority topics identified by their colleagues (TC3). To engage the staff, the program leadership team and Early CHOICES designed a brief electronic survey to determine the topics for this next day in the series and to recruit staff interested in facilitating discussions and/or sharing strategies about a topic (TC2). Staff were encouraged to think about topics that relate to the ICP and their role and to identify their strengths to share (TC2). Respondents expressed an interest in a variety of inclusive practices, including supporting engagement in free choice and group activities, facilitating communication among the children, and providing supports for children who have not attended school before.

Nine ARECC staff volunteered to facilitate 20-minute coffee talks. The staff facilitators hosted the coffee talks in their classrooms so that they could share any relevant resources they already had in place. Staff selected three coffee talks from the nine topics to attend and were able to engage with peers and hear from the facilitator (TC2). The talks provided opportunities to discuss and share strategies to address the priority areas identified by their team (TC1, TC2, TC3). Early CHOICES attended the talks to observe the process, to learn, and to take notes as needed. To build on the program's strengths and facilitate a shared understanding, all of the conversations, strategies, and questions were documented in a shared online format with all staff (TC1, TC2, TC3). Staff comments reinforced the value of having colleagues as facilitators of professional learning; they felt it extended engagement and encouraged implementation. For example, staff said "I have not been in another classroom in a long time," "I would love to do the same format again so I could attend all of the sessions," and "I was thrilled to have a chance to ask a question about the new behavior intervention strategies that we started." To finish the experience, the entire staff formed a circle and called out one practice that they were inspired to use in their classrooms (TC3).

Early CHOICES developed and distributed an anonymous electronic survey to evaluate the series. Most staff reported they wanted more time to engage collaboratively with their peers and that teaming had positive outcomes for their practices (TC1, TC2, TC3). Another theme among participants was a need for more opportunities to dive deeper into the practices within the ICP. One respondent commented:

> Of course, time is always at a premium. I would have loved to spend more time observing in my classroom using the tool. Even by

"

Most staff reported they wanted more time to engage collaboratively with their peers and that teaming had positive outcomes for their practices.

delegating different sections to various team members, it felt like I was barely able to scratch the surface in the time allotted.

Based on the responses from participants, Early CHOICES and ARECC have agreed to continue the professional learning series into a second year. The work will expand to include families more intentionally because this series did not focus enough on engaging families in collaboration. For example, the program team could use the routine-based activity planning matrix to connect with families regarding school routines and encourage their input about their children's strengths and interests (TC5). In addition, this can encourage families to share what they need to support their children at home, allowing the program to partner to meet those needs or connect the families with community resources (TC4).

Key Factors That Supported This Professional Learning Series

To develop this yearlong professional learning series, Early CHOICES staff used what we knew about using a team-based model of change and best practices in professional learning. We drew upon our collective experiences as former teachers, home visitors, and technical assistance providers trained to reliability with the ICP. We used strong, practical tools to support self-reflection, including *The Preschool Inclusion Toolbox* (Barton & Smith, 2015); "What Makes Inclusion Work" (Early CHOICES, n.d.-c), a self-reflection tool based on the ICP; and videos from high-quality classrooms (Early CHOICES, n.d.-a).

External factors created the right climate for this work and supported this endeavor and contributed to its success as well. The ICP provided us with a tool to create innovative professional learning based on its practices. At the state level, Illinois shows a commitment to inclusion in several ways: embedding inclusion in the state QRIS, developing inclusion guidance from the state board of education, and funding Early CHOICES, a project dedicated to training and technical assistance on inclusion in early childhood. At the local level, the program with which we collaborated had infrastructure in place to support professional learning and leadership strongly committed to inclusion.

Teaming and collaboration occurred among the entire staff because the administrative team and all staff members participated in all dates of the series and because the series was designed collaboratively with the administrative team to incorporate the DEC Recommended Practices to maximize opportunities for engagement.

References

Bailey, D. B., McWilliam, P. J., & Winton, P. J. (1992). Building family-centered practices in early intervention: A team-based model for change. *Infants and Young Children, 5*(1), 73–82.

Barton, E. E., & Smith, B. J. (2015). *The preschool inclusion toolbox: How to build and lead a high-quality program.* Baltimore, MD: Paul H. Brookes.

Bricker, D., Pretti-Frontczak, K., & McComas, N. (1998). *An activity-based approach to early intervention* (2nd ed.). Baltimore, MD: Paul H. Brookes.

DEC/NAEYC. (2009). *Early childhood inclusion: A joint position statement of the Division for Early Childhood (DEC) and the National Association for the Education of Young Children (NAEYC).* Chapel Hill: The University of North Carolina, FPG Child Development Institute.

Division for Early Childhood. (2014). *DEC recommended practices in early intervention/early childhood special education 2014.* Retrieved from http://www.dec-sped.org/dec-recommended-practices

Early CHOICES. (n.d.-a). Early CHOICES [YouTube Channel]. Retrieved from www.youtube.com/channel/UCIfVTAREF2X-9-BTZiZuOHg/featured

Early CHOICES. (n.d.-b). Using the ICP for self-reflection. Retrieved from https://www.livebinders.com/play/play?id=1937670

Early CHOICES. (n.d.-c). What makes inclusion work. Retrieved from http://www.eclre.org/good-to-know/what-makes-inclusion-work.aspx

Early CHOICES. (2017). ICP self-reflection. Retrieved from http://www.eclre.org/media/138170/icp-personal-reflection-tool2017.pdf

Eby, L. T., Adams, D. M., Russell, J. E., & Gaby, S. H. (2000). Perceptions of organizational readiness for change: Factors related to employees' reactions to the implementation of team-based selling. *Human Relations, 53,* 419–442. doi:10.1177/0018726700533006

Fixen, D. L., Naoom, S. F., Blase, K. A., Friedman, R. M., & Wallace, F. (2005). *Implementation research: A synthesis of the literature* (FMHI Publication No. 231). Tampa: University of South Florida, Louis de la Parte Florida Mental Health Institute, The National Implementation Research Network.

Joyce, B., & Calhoun, E. (2010). *Models of professional development: A celebration of educators.* Thousand Oaks, CA: Corwin Press.

Joyce, B., & Showers, B. (2002). *Student achievement through staff development* (3rd ed.). Alexandria, VA: Association for Supervision and Curriculum Development.

National Professional Development Center on Inclusion. (2008). *What do we mean by professional development in the early childhood field?* Chapel Hill: The University of North Carolina, FPG Child Development Institute.

Snyder, P., Hemmeter, M. L., & McLaughlin, T. (2011). Professional development in early childhood intervention: Where we stand on the silver anniversary of PL 99-457. *Journal of Early Intervention, 33,* 357–370. doi:10.1177/1053815111428336

Soukakou, E. P. (2012). Measuring quality in inclusive preschool classrooms: Development and validation of the inclusive classroom profile (ICP). *Early Childhood Research Quarterly, 27,* 478–488. doi:10.1016/j.ecresq.2011.12.003

Soukakou, E. P., Winton, P. J., West, T. A., Sideris, J. H., & Rucker, L. M. (2014). Measuring the quality of inclusive practices: Findings from the inclusive classroom profile pilot. *Journal of Early Intervention, 36,* 223–240. doi:10.1177/1053815115569732

State Implementation and Scaling-up of Evidence-based Practices. (n.d.). Retrieved from https://sisep.fpg.unc.edu/about

U.S. Department of Health and Human Services & U.S. Department of Education. (2015, September 14). *Policy statement on inclusion of children with disabilities in early childhood programs.* Retrieved from https://ed.gov/policy/speced/guid/earlylearning/joint-statement-full-text.pdf

Winton, P. J., McWilliam, P. J., Harrison, T., Owens, A. M., & Bailey, D. B. (1992). Lessons learned from implementing a team-based model for change. *Infants and Young Children, 5*(1), 49–57. doi:10.1097/00001163-199207000-00008

10

The Power of Teams
Time to Move Forward in Interprofessional Personnel Preparation

Jennifer L. Kilgo
Laura Vogtle
Jerry Aldridge
William Ronilo
University of Alabama at Birmingham

Faculty members representing multiple disciplines at an urban university have focused their research and service on young children with delays or disabilities. They recently connected with one another at a state conference and discussed the statewide need to better prepare early childhood personnel to work as team members. They realized that collectively they had both expertise and interest and decided they wanted to develop an interdisciplinary graduate program. They know there will be numerous steps in the process and challenges to address within their university. How will they collaboratively develop an interprofessional program when the programs are in different schools and departments? Will administrators in each school and department support teaching hours and responsibilities outside of previously scheduled coursework and other faculty responsibilities? Negotiating faculty and program expectations, as well as accreditation concerns, across departments in a large university is no small task. Generating interest in students who carry large credit loads is an additional issue. In addition, many students work full time and attend classes part time, as is often the case in early childhood special education. The faculty realize external funding may be necessary to provide scholarships and support the additional responsibilities to faculty workloads.

Aside from practical concerns, there will be philosophical issues. Clearly the legislation governing the delivery of early intervention/early childhood special education (EC/ECSE) needs to be foundational to the planned program, as do priorities of federal and state agencies and national organizations. Practical factors need to be considered as well. How do local agencies deliver team-based services, and what are the families' perspectives? Throughout this article, suggestions for resolution of such issues are provided.

Rationale for Interprofessional Programs

Interprofessional or interdisciplinary programs in higher education designed to prepare personnel representing multiple disciplines to serve early intervention/early childhood special education (EI/ECSE) populations are critical to building a high-quality workforce (Stayton, 2015). For years, EI/ECSE leaders have called for an interdisciplinary approach in personnel preparation (Bailey, 1996; Bailey, Simeonsson, Yoder, & Huntington, 1990; Bruder, 2010; Kilgo & Bruder, 1997). While some higher education programs have embraced the notion of interprofessional education (Barton, Moore, & Squires, 2012; Campbell, Chiarello, Wilcox, & Milbourne, 2009), much work remains. Limited empirical information is available regarding programs that address interdisciplinary teaming content in general and those that prepare students from multiple disciplines in interdisciplinary programs in particular (Bruder, 2016; Stayton, 2015). Advancements are needed to bridge the gap between evidence-based teaming practices and interprofessional education that results in improved outcomes for graduates to become effective team members (Bruder, 2016; Bruder & Dunst, 2005; Mellin & Winton, 2003; Stayton, 2015).

The purpose of this article is to provide strategies to faculty who are interested in developing or enhancing existing interprofessional graduate programs. This article draws recommendations from an interprofessional graduate program, Project TransTeam, that has been in operation for more than two decades at the University of Alabama at Birmingham (UAB). It is focused on the preparation of students from early childhood special education (ECSE), physical therapy (PT), and occupational therapy (OT). The article begins with a description of the multiple factors that influenced the development of this interprofessional program, followed by an overview of the teaming content, processes, requirements, structure, and evaluation of Project TransTeam. The article concludes with recommendations for moving forward in interprofessional education.

Interprofessional Education Influences and Framework

Project TransTeam builds on the work of leaders in the EI/ECSE field that provided recommendations many years ago for interdisciplinary personnel preparation programs, both content and processes (Bailey, 1996; Thorp & McCollum, 1994). In developing the content of Project TransTeam, faculty incorporated the philosophical changes that have occurred in EI/ECSE, such as the movement to family-centered services and the provision of services in natural environments, which support the need for interprofessional personnel preparation (see Figure 1). In addition, the faculty considered legislation that has called for the practice of employing teams in special education since the passage of P.L. 94-142. Another factor was the U.S. Department of Education's Office of Special Education Program (OSEP) priorities that have provided funding to encourage university personnel preparation programs to provide interprofessional training and address team development and functioning (Stayton, 2015). Further influencing the interprofessional focus of Project TransTeam were the recommendations from professional organizations such as the Division

> The faculty participating in the pilot program shared common interests and experiences in working with young children with delays or disabilities; however, each discipline was addressing the EI/ECSE content inconsistently and in a cursory manner.

Figure 1

Philosophical Trends in EI/ECSE Influencing Interprofessional Personnel Preparation

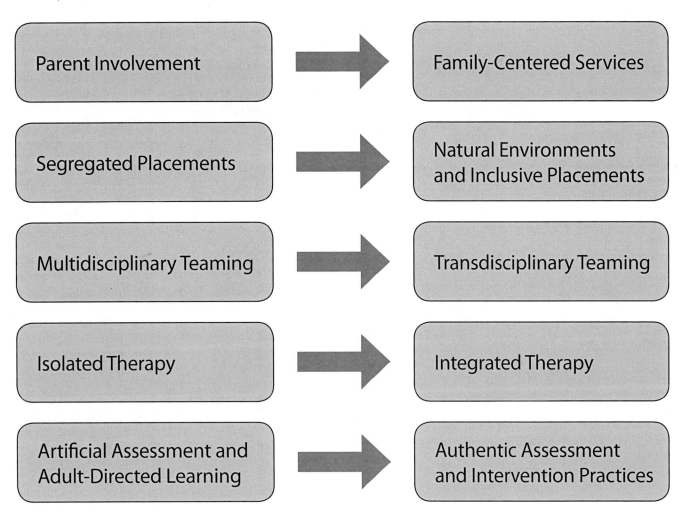

for Early Childhood (DEC) Recommended Practices, as well as other professional organizations (e.g., American Physical Therapy Association, American Occupational Therapy Association, American Speech and Hearing Association). Figure 2 illustrates the influences and potential outcomes of interprofessional personnel preparation.

Framework for Developing an Interprofessional Program

Project TransTeam began as a pilot program at UAB almost 20 years ago with faculty from early childhood special education (ECSE), general early childhood education (ECE), and occupational and physical therapies (OT, PT). Like the faculty members in the vignette, the faculty participating in the pilot program shared common interests and experiences in working with young children with delays or disabilities; however, each discipline was addressing the EI/ECSE content inconsistently and in a cursory manner in the related service curricula. The faculty realized the difficulty in successfully acquiring federal funding for their

Figure 2

Influences and Outcomes of Interprofessional Personnel Preparation in EI/ECSE

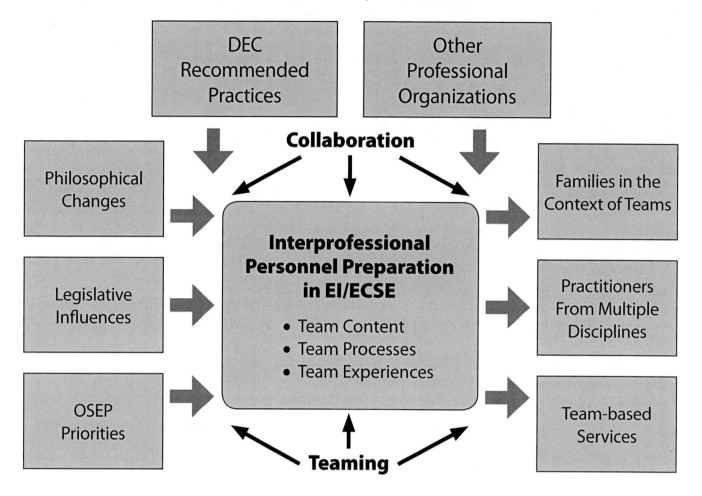

interprofessional program and first sought university financial support for the development of the pilot program (i.e., faculty release time, funding for planning meetings, interprofessional training materials). They also garnered local community support in several ways. They invited EI/ECSE practitioners and administrators to help develop the pilot program and conducted a community needs assessment.

With financial support from the departments and assistance from community collaborators who participated in the planning process and coursework, the pilot program began. The program consisted of two courses that were open to students from three programs (ECSE, PT, OT). Using information learned from the pilot program, the faculty began seeking external funding. For example, the faculty learned that one of the most difficult obstacles they faced was scheduling coursework, which resulted in courses taught in the late afternoon/early evening. The faculty also determined that it was most effective for students to enroll in the interdisciplinary courses during their second year after they had acquired discipline-specific information. The pilot program helped determine the cross-disciplinary content, the team-based instructional practices, and team-based assignments. Beginning in 2002, they successfully secured 15 years of continuous federally funded personnel preparation grants from OSEP with another five-year cycle that began in 2017. These grant awards provide not only student scholarships but salary support to faculty, which enables them to have release time to work on the program.

Project TransTeam provides graduate students representing ECSE, PT, and OT with learning experiences alongside students from other disciplines. Project TransTeam faculty members include an early childhood special educator, occupational therapist, physical therapist, and general early childhood educator. Parents of young children with disabilities also participate in the interprofessional courses as coteachers and panel members with stipends provided through the Project TransTeam grant. Practitioners from other disciplines (speech-language pathology, nursing, public health) and teams from the community contribute to the courses as well by participating on panels and serving as consultants to the students as they work on their course assignments. Faculty members have established partnerships with many exemplary programs and schools in the community. Team members from these programs and schools, many of whom are Project TransTeam alumni, contribute their time to the interprofessional courses by participating on panels and serving as guest lecturers. Including families, teachers, therapists, and administrators from local EI/ECSE agencies in coursework provides students with perspectives on the day-to-day realities of teamwork, such as communication, scheduling, problem-solving, role release, resources, and family experiences. The faculty give back to the community by serving on local advisory boards, providing community-based professional development, and helping with evaluation activities.

Through Project TransTeam, graduate students from multiple disciplines receive scholarships. The ECSE students receive scholarships for two years because their entire program focuses on EI/ECSE; the OT and PT students are awarded scholarships for the one year that their programs focus on EI/ECSE. The OT, PT, and ECSE students are educated together in courses and participate in ongoing team-based field experiences. Students participate in this interprofessional coursework during their second year of graduate school. They enroll in one shared interprofessional course per semester as well as complete pediatric courses and EI/ECSE field experiences throughout the program. The shared course offered during the first semester is Foundations of Transdisciplinary Teaming in EI/ECSE, and the shared course in the second semester is Transdisciplinary Teaming Processes in EI/ECSE. Both are offered in the late afternoon/early evening to be available to students in full-time programs and those who work full time and attend classes. (Copies of the interprofessional course syllabi are available from the first author of this article.)

Because faculty members and community stakeholders (family members, ECSE teachers, therapists, agency leaders) participate in the interprofessional courses, students learn about the expertise and services other disciplines can offer. Teams of professionals from the community share their roles, responsibilities, and practices through panel discussions, and they interact and consult with students on the team-based assignments. The community involvement in the courses ensures students are exposed to high-quality teams of professionals,

> Including families, teachers, therapists, and administrators from local EI/ECSE agencies in coursework provides students with perspectives on the day-to-day realities of teamwork.

and it provides linkages for transdisciplinary field experiences in which students complete assignments and observe the professionals.

Interprofessional Content, Processes, and Experiences

In addition to cross-disciplinary content from areas (legislation, family-centered practices, cultural responsiveness, inclusion, team assessment, evidence-based practices, and transdisciplinary service delivery approach) that are applicable to all disciplines involved in EI/ECSE, Project TransTeam focuses on the direct applicability of the training to prepare students for future roles and responsibilities on teams. Graduate students actively engage with one another in the courses as opportunities are provided to practice teaming and collaboration skills such as problem-solving, conflict resolution, joint decision-making, role release, group facilitation, and communication.

Project TransTeam uses teaching processes that address the Teaming and Collaboration recommended practices. DEC emphasizes the importance of practices that "promote and sustain collaborative adult partnerships, relationships, and ongoing interactions" among members of the team (DEC, 2016, p. 29). Table 1 provides the Teaming and Collaboration recommended practices and summarizes how each practice is addressed in the interprofessional coursework (DEC, 2014) as described in greater detail below.

The interprofessional courses are taught using an interactive format designed to foster active engagement and interaction among students and faculty. During the first semester of the Project TransTeam courses, students learn about the roles of the various disciplines on the team and specific content needed by all disciplines to serve on EI/ECSE teams. They learn to use communication and facilitation practices that enhance team functioning and support relationships. One of the primary teaching methods used by Project TransTeam faculty is case-based instruction, which has grown rapidly as a viable means to prepare students to develop skills applied to realistic situations in EI/ECSE settings (Snyder & McWilliam, 2003). Case-based instruction requires learners to actively participate in situations that reflect the kind of experiences naturally encountered and prepares them for what they will experience in their future roles by exposing them to similar situations and issues during the instruction.

Project TransTeam faculty have developed a three-phase model of case-based instruction that has evolved over time. During the first years of Project TransTeam, students were immediately introduced to complex cases; however, they often had difficulty attending to all the variables necessary to address such complex cases. The faculty modified the case-based instruction by dividing the process into three types of cases, or what eventually developed into the three-phase model. From what the faculty had learned, they determined that the first experiences with case-based instruction should involve problem-solving with unidimensional vignettes. These vignettes are composed of just one major element of diversity as students solve problems around family structure diversity, then religious diversity, and finally ethnic diversity. Examples of each type of vignette can be found in Table 2.

Of course, there are often multiple issues involved in working with families,

Case-based instruction requires learners to actively participate in situations that reflect the kind of experiences naturally encountered and prepares them for what they will experience in their future roles.

Table 1

Examples of How the Teaming and Collaboration Recommended Practices Are Addressed in the Project TransTeam Courses

Recommended practice	How it is addressed
TC1. Practitioners representing multiple disciplines and families work together as a team to plan and implement supports and services to meet the unique needs of each child and family.	Students are provided with multiple opportunities to assume roles and responsibilities as members of interdisciplinary teams as they complete assignments using case studies. During the second semester, the teams engage in planning and apply teaming strategies as they address the issues in complex cases. The students learn to collaborate with and provide support and feedback to other disciplines.
TC2. Practitioners and families work together as a team to systematically and regularly exchange expertise, knowledge, and information to build team capacity and jointly solve problems, plan, and implement interventions.	The student teams participate in ongoing problem-solving as they engage in planning (assessment, outcomes/goals development, evidence-based intervention, transitions). They provide interprofessional support as they work as a team to complete the requirements of the case assignments.
TC3. Practitioners use communication and group facilitation strategies to enhance team functioning and interpersonal relationships with and among team members.	In the interdisciplinary courses, students develop interpersonal relationships with students from other disciplines as they interact on teams. They are given multiple opportunities to develop and use communication and group facilitation strategies to enhance team functioning through activities and assignments.
TC4. Team members assist each other to discover and access community-based services and other informal and formal resources to meet family-identified child or family needs.	When problem solving to address the needs identified in the case studies, the teams of students are required to collaboratively determine community services and resources for children and families. Family members from the community explain the importance of family-identified child and family needs and provide feedback to students as they determine formal and informal supports.
TC5. Practitioners and families may collaborate with each other to identify one practitioner from the team who serves as the primary liaison between the family and other team members based on child and family priorities and needs.	As teams of students work on the complex cases, they must collaboratively determine the primary family liaison. They use a problem-solving process based on the child and the priorities and needs identified by the family.

Table 2
Examples of Unidimensional and Multidimensional Vignettes for Problem-Solving

Examples of unidimensional vignettes

Family structures

Your team is working with a family in which there is joint custody, where the father has the child for a week and the mother has him for the next week. Their goals for the child are contradictory and each parent does NOT want the team to work on the goals of the other family member. What would your team do?

Religious diversity

A family is part of a charismatic Catholic community. The major goal for their child with arthrogryposis is to take him to a sacred place in Mexico for healing. How would your team work with the family on goals for the child?

Ethnic diversity

Your team is working with a family from Japan. The family is highly resistant to meeting in the home. How (and where) would the team work with the child and family? Why?

Example of a multidimensional vignette

- Sara and Jamal (male) are 33-month-old fraternal twins who were born prematurely. Both are developmentally delayed with indications of cerebral palsy. Sara is the more "involved" child in terms of cognitive, physical, and language development.
- The parents are devout Muslims from Oman. At the first team meeting, the father is clearly the spokesman for the family. He said he does not talk to women about his children's development or future education. However, there are no men on the team.
- His goals for Jamal are also clear. The father wants support for Jamal to be able to request what he wants in Arabic. He also wants Jamal to learn his colors. Finally, he wants Jamal to receive occupational therapy to help him learn to feed himself and physical therapy to "learn to walk."
- Even though Sara is more involved, he does not want any services for her because she is a girl.

What would your team do in this situation?

and teaming can be impacted by diverse cultural influences (Aldridge, Kilgo, & Bruton, 2016). Therefore, after problem solving with the unidimensional vignettes, the second phase of case-based instruction is introduced, which is composed of multidimensional vignettes. For example, the students consider what to do if families advocate for practices that conflict with other team members' values or if their goals are inconsistent with program or school policies. Students work as teams to develop plans based on the families' values, priorities, and goals.

Finally, in the second semester of the Project TransTeam courses, students are assigned to teams of five to six students representing multiple disciplines. Each team is assigned a complex case study, which is the third phase of the case-based instruction model. Each complex case study describes a young child who qualifies for services under IDEA. The Project TransTeam faculty collaboratively develop the cases and modify them each semester, based on student feedback. The complex cases require the expertise of a team representing various disciplines and present several aspects of diversity and multifaceted issues to be addressed by the student teams at different transition points (e.g., referral to EI, moving from EI to preschool services). The comprehensive case studies involve weekly activities that extend for a full semester and serve as a culminating assignment. As a team, the students practice communication skills and strategies for sharing knowledge and expertise as they explore the case studies and design appropriate goals, interventions, and services. (A portfolio of cases is available from the first author of this article upon request.) A portion of one of the comprehensive cases follows.

A group of educators and related service professionals (e.g., PT, OT, SLP) is charged with supporting a 33-month-old boy named Diego with an easy temperament and a diagnosis of cerebral palsy. He was born at 26 weeks with a birth weight of 1,300 grams. He has hydrocephalus with a grade 3 interventricular hemorrhage (IVH) bilaterally and a permanent ventriculoperitoneal shunt that was implanted at 5 weeks of age. Diego's family is from Honduras. Due to the tragic death of his mother from complications of childbirth, Diego lives with his maternal grandmother, who speaks Spanish fluently but no English and stays at home with Diego and his aunt, who speaks limited English and is the primary income provider. Diego's aunt soon may be laid off and wants Diego and his grandmother to return to Honduras until she can find work.

Diego is transitioning from early intervention to preschool services. Each professional conducted an assessment and developed goals in the domains associated with their respective disciplines. The early childhood special educator can offer suggestions for meeting Diego's educational needs, but she does not understand the specific implications of his physical and health care needs. The therapists can suggest ways to address his gross motor, fine motor, and communication skills through therapy, but they have limited knowledge of how to integrate these recommendations into the learning environment. They are struggling with how to support Diego's grandmother and include her as part of the team. In short, they lack training about each other's disciplines, the types of services they could provide, how to function as a team, and the synergy they might experience working as a team.

Workplace situations such as those described in Diego's case happen every day. Unless practitioners from multiple disciplines can work effectively with young children with significant needs such as Diego, they will not provide the help Diego needs to develop and thrive. For Diego and his family, several issues were identified in the case for the student teams to address: (a) placement in an appropriate preschool with peers, taking into consideration the family's funding limitations and possible future unemployment; (b) seating and positioning as it relates to mobility, activities of daily living, play, safety, etc.; (c) modifications and adaptations for play and communication; (d) language barriers between home, preschool, and service providers; (e) language barrier between Diego and his new

The complex cases require the expertise of a team representing various disciplines and present several aspects of diversity and multifaceted issues to be addressed by the student teams at different transition points.

caregivers; (f) access to outside resources (therapies, medical clinics, community and monetary support groups); and (g) immigration and service issues if Diego and his grandmother leave the country.

Students are required to function as transdisciplinary teams as they develop plans to respond to the cases. Each week of the seminar focuses on a different aspect of the cases. Team-based learning occurs as the student teams complete each component of the case in written reports. These are presented orally and discussed with the class. They describe the following: (a) setting, service delivery model, team members and characteristics, and available human resources; (b) the child and family, including the family social history, family strengths, history of child and the delay or disability, community support and services available, and cultural considerations and/or adaptations needed; (c) roles and responsibilities of each discipline, including the primary provider; (d) assessment instruments and processes (formal, informal, team-based); (e) Individualized Family Service Plan (IFSP) and Individual Education Program (IEP), with clear evidence of opportunities for family input; (f) strategies to meet outcomes and goals with explanations for choices of strategies, the evidence to support the intervention strategies, and an explanation of how team members will carry out the intervention strategies; (g) formal and informal resources; (h) how the team will address the specific issues identified in the case; (i) plan for transitions from EI and preschool; and (j) how the team functioned and the team's overall effectiveness.

The complex cases are hypothetical, and some information must be developed by the student teams. For example, the cases identify the religious and socioeconomic backgrounds of the families; however, the students must conduct research to learn more about the impact of these factors on the issues identified in their case study. When teams of students work together to develop all components of the cases and focus on the issues and challenges, multiple opportunities for team learning occur. Students engage in collaborative processes and apply the teaming skills they have learned through the interprofessional courses. During the culminating class meetings, the student teams present their cases to the class, answer questions, and lead the discussion regarding the issues identified in their cases. Both students and faculty representing multiple disciplines participate in the discussion and provide feedback on the cases. Although the courses provide many occasions to simulate team experiences, opportunities also are available for students to experience teams in action (assessments, team meetings, intervention) as they complete assignments and requirements in field settings and receive ongoing feedback.

Monitoring Effectiveness and Outcomes

Ultimately, the success of interprofessional education is determined by its effectiveness and outcomes. The Project TransTeam faculty evaluate the extent to which the graduates master competencies and essential team-based practices, the program's effectiveness, and the program's impact on the local community and EI/ECSE workforce. During the program, data from each cohort is collected to assess the effectiveness of the program to make improvements for future

When teams of students work together to develop all components of the cases and focus on the issues and challenges, multiple opportunities for team learning occur.

cohorts. These data include pre- and postprogram self-assessments that address cross-disciplinary competency areas with comparisons of these data across and between disciplines. In addition, students are asked to provide open-ended feedback at the end of each semester. Results from this feedback are reviewed by the faculty to make changes in future courses. After completing the comprehensive case assignment in the second semester, all student team members rate and provide feedback to the other team members on their effectiveness as team members using a peer assessment rubric. In addition, each student is required to complete a paper that summarizes the processes and practices, both positive and challenging; their team's work on the case studies; and their effectiveness as a team. The papers are shared and discussed to explore different perspectives on the teaming experience.

In Project TransTeam, student skill attainment in the program's competencies, which include the DEC Recommended Practices (2014) and emphasize the Teaming and Collaboration practices, is measured in several ways. In addition to

feedback and grades on projects and field-based requirements, students complete a postprogram self-assessment measure that includes program competencies and identifies critical skills in implementing the Teaming and Collaboration recommended practices. On this self-assessment rubric, which is based on a four-point Likert scale, 70% of the 19 students from PT, OT, and ECSE in the 2017–2018 Project TransTeam cohort rated themselves as 3 (skilled) or 4 (highly skilled) on all five Teaming and Collaboration recommended practices. The recommended practice that received the lowest rating was TC4,

which focuses on collaborating to secure resources, with 47% of the 19 students rating themselves as 3 (skilled) and 53% rating themselves as 4 (highly skilled). One explanation is that perhaps it takes many years of practice before practitioners feel highly skilled in collaborating to secure resources. This is an area that the Project TransTeam faculty review and make necessary improvements in the training for students.

The Project TransTeam faculty team routinely reviews the evaluation process, explores options, and improves the evaluation methods and tools. Updates to pre–post self-assessment and follow-up measures were made to improve the information collected after talking with faculty from other interprofessional programs and receiving objective feedback by external evaluators. The goal is to deliver effective interprofessional education that produces graduates who are well prepared to serve as team members; thus, the value of monitoring the effectiveness and outcomes of interprofessional preservice programs cannot be overstated (Bruder, 2016). Because the success of this program is determined by its effectiveness in preparing students with the knowledge and ability to function as team members, follow-up feedback from students and other stakeholders (employers, families, field supervisors) is gathered each year (both during and following the program). The following example of feedback from a graduate student suggests that Project TransTeam is succeeding:

> We were prepared to implement a transdisciplinary model by working with team members representing different disciplines. We learned from each other, developed team-based goals, determined appropriate interventions, and found the best available evidence as a team. The team assignments allowed us to put trust in each other and to effectively communicate, problem solve, and sometimes compromise to work through our complex case studies, which is what working as a transdisciplinary team requires. (Project TransTeam graduate student, 2017)

Moving Forward

In closing, we stress the need for innovative interprofessional preservice programs in higher education to ensure that teaming and collaboration are emphasized for all disciplines involved in EI/ECSE. Hopefully, what we have learned through Project TransTeam will be a resource for those who want to (a) implement an interprofessional education approach, (b) prepare graduates who are well qualified to serve as members of teams, and (c) address the Teaming and Collaboration recommended practices. As we move forward in interprofessional education, we recommend that faculty in higher education programs:

- Expand the interprofessional EI/ECSE focus in preservice education;
- Invest in innovative ways to address the Teaming and Collaboration recommended practices in interprofessional personnel preparation programs;
- Consider using case-based instruction to teach the Teaming and Collaboration recommended practices;
- Expand and improve the ways to measure teaching effectiveness, teaming skills, and team-based learning (content and processes) in interprofessional education; and
- Invest in the development of better evaluation measures and processes that are linked to the effectiveness of graduates as team members in demonstrating team-based competencies (during and following preservice education).

Expanding interprofessional education in EI/ECSE, evaluating the effectiveness of these efforts (content, processes, experiences), and collaborating with other colleges and universities will help advance research, knowledge, and practices in personnel preparation programs. Ultimately, exemplary interprofessional education will improve team-based services that will benefit young children, families, and professionals.

References

Aldridge, J., Kilgo, J. L., & Bruton, A. K. (2016). Beyond the Brady Bunch: Hybrid families and their evolving relationships with early childhood educators. *Childhood Education, 92*, 140–148. doi:10.1080/00094056.2016.1150752

Bailey, D. B., Jr. (1996). An overview of interdisciplinary teaching. In D. Bricker & A. Widerstrom (Eds.), *Preparing personnel to work with infants and young children and their families: A team approach* (pp. 67–90). Baltimore, MD: Paul H. Brookes.

Bailey, D. B., Jr., Simeonsson, R. J., Yoder, D. E., & Huntington G. S. (1990). Preparing professionals to serve infants and toddlers with handicaps and their families: An integrative analysis across eight disciplines. *Exceptional Children, 57*, 26–35. doi:10.1177/001440299005700104

Barton, E. E., Moore, H. W., & Squires, J. K. (2012). Preparing speech language pathology students to work in early childhood. *Topics in Early Childhood Special Education, 32*, 4–13. doi:10.1177/0271121411434567

Bruder, M. B. (2010). Early childhood intervention: A promise to children and families for their future. *Exceptional Children, 76*, 339–355. doi:10.1177/001440291007600306

Bruder, M. B. (2016). Personnel development practices in early childhood intervention. In B. Reichow, B. A. Boyd, E. E. Barton, & S. L. Odom (Eds.), *Handbook of early childhood special education* (pp. 289–333). Cham, Switzerland: Springer.

Bruder, M. B., & Dunst C. J. (2005). Personnel preparation in recommended early intervention practices: Degree of emphasis across disciplines. *Topics in Early Childhood Special Education, 25*, 25–33. doi:10.1177/02711214050250010301

Campbell, P. H., Chiarello, L., Wilcox, M. J., & Milbourne, S. (2009). Preparing therapists as effective practitioners in early intervention. *Infants & Young Children, 22*, 21–31. doi:10.1097/01.IYC.0000343334.26904.92

Division for Early Childhood. (2014). *DEC recommended practices in early intervention/early childhood special education 2014.* Retrieved from http://www.dec-sped.org/dec-recommended-practices

Division of Early Childhood. (2016). *DEC recommended practices in early intervention/early childhood special education with examples.* Retrieved from http://www.dec-sped.org/dec-recommended-practices

Kilgo, J. L., & Bruder, M. B. (1997). Creating new visions in institutions of higher education: Interdisciplinary approaches to personnel preparation in early intervention. In P. J. Winton, J. A. McCollum, & C. Catlett (Eds.), *Reforming personnel preparation in early intervention: Issues, models, and practical strategies* (pp. 81–102). Baltimore, MD: Paul H. Brookes.

Mellin, A. E., & Winton, P. J. (2003). Interdisciplinary collaboration among early intervention faculty members. *Journal of Early Intervention, 25*, 173–188. doi:10.1177/105381510302500303

Snyder, P., & McWilliam, P. J. (2003). Using case method of instruction effectively in early intervention personnel preparation. *Infants & Young Children, 16*, 284–295.

Stayton, V. D. (2015). Preparation of early childhood special educators for inclusive and interdisciplinary settings. *Infants & Young Children, 28,* 113–122. doi:10.1097/IYC.0000000000000030

Thorp, E. K., & McCollum, J. A. (1994). Defining the infancy specialization in early childhood special education. In L. J. Johnson, R. J. Gallagher, M. J. LaMontagne, J. B. Jordan, & J. J. Gallagher (Eds.), *Meeting early intervention challenges: Issues from birth to three* (pp. 167–183). Baltimore, MD: Paul H. Brookes.

11

Resources to Support Teaming and Collaboration Practices

CHIH-ING LIM
Frank Porter Graham Child Development Institute

SHUTING ZHENG
University of California, San Francisco

I T TAKES A VILLAGE TO RAISE A CHILD. FOR YOUNG CHILDREN WHO HAVE or are at risk for developmental delays and disabilities, their village includes not only their family and school or child care but also practitioners who come from multiple disciplines and agencies with different values, regulations, and procedures. It is therefore critical for practitioners to have the confidence and competence to "promote and sustain collaborative adult partnerships, relationships, and ongoing interactions to ensure that programs and services achieve desired child and family outcomes and goals" (Division for Early Childhood, 2014, p. 15). The goal of this article is to provide early childhood, early intervention, and early childhood special education practitioners; higher education faculty; and professional development providers with resources that they can use to enhance their knowledge and skills on using the Teaming and Collaboration recommended practices. All the resources included in this article are available at no charge.

Overview of How Resources Are Organized

The annotated compendium of resources in this article complements the information provided by the articles in this monograph. We begin with a collection of general resources on teaming and collaboration practices that addresses the recommended practices comprehensively. This is followed by resources that address specific strategies on communication for collaboration and supporting families as essential members of the team, respectively. Finally, evaluation and self-assessment tools for teaming and collaboration are provided.

General Resources

Collaboration With Families and Other Partners: Essential Features of High-Quality Inclusion

This archived webinar is part of a series of four webinars jointly presented by staff from the Office of Special Education Programs (OSEP) and the Office of Head Start (OHS). It provides information on federal laws and policies and resources related to building partnerships that ensure high-quality inclusion for children with disabilities. Strategies for collaborating with state and community partners to build stronger infrastructure supports are also discussed. Included as part of this resource is an analysis of IDEA Part C and B requirements related to family engagement. *Developers: Early Childhood Technical Assistance Center (ECTA) and the National Center for Early Childhood Development, Teaching, and Learning with funding from OSEP and OHS*

> https://eclkc.ohs.acf.hhs.gov/video/
> collaboration-families-other-partners-essential-features-high-quality-inclusion

IEP Videos

This series of videos can be used to guide practitioners and families who might be new to IEP meetings to know what an IEP meeting might look like and how they may prepare for it. The videos include examples of setting up, beginning, and wrapping up the meeting. The resource also provides an example of how family members and service providers can work together to set intervention goals and education plans. *Developer: Head Start Center for Inclusion*

> http://headstartinclusion.org/iep-videos

Joint Policy Statement on the Collaboration and Coordination of the Maternal, Infant, and Early Childhood Home Visiting Program (MIECHV) and the Individuals With Disabilities Education Act (IDEA) Part C Program

This joint policy statement provides recommendations for states and local communities to provide coordinated MIECHV and IDEA Part C program services for the most vulnerable families and children to connect them to the array of services they need to enhance both family functioning as well as children's development and learning. Based on interviews with 10 states that have been working to strengthen MIECHV awardee and IDEA Part C state program partnerships, a total of eight recommendations are generated along with examples of successful partnerships. *Developers: U.S. Department of Education and the U.S. Department of Health and Human Services*

> https://www2.ed.gov/about/inits/ed/earlylearning/files/ed-hhs-miechv-partc-
> guidance.pdf

Leading by Convening: A Blueprint for Authentic Engagement

This blueprint provides a framework for leaders at all levels to engage with stakeholders effectively. The framework has three key elements: coalescing around issues, ensuring relevant participation, and doing the work together. While the blueprint is targeted at national, state, or district level leaders to encourage them to come together to solve common problems, it is also relevant for local teams. For example, it provides strategies for valuing diverse perspectives, making shared decisions, and ensuring common vocabulary among multidisciplinary or cross-agency personnel and families. *Developers: Joanne Cashman, Patrice Cunniff Linehan, Luann Purcell, Mariola Rosser, Sharon Schultz, and Stacy Skalski with funding from OSEP*

> http://www.ideapartnership.org/documents/NovUploads/Leading%20by%20Convening%20508.pdf

Practitioner Practice Guide 3.1: Team Members Helping One Another Learn and Grow

Because practitioners serving young children with disabilities and their families often have to work in interdisciplinary and interagency teams, it is important that team members learn different perspectives and knowledge and develop better professional skills together. This practice guide helps practitioners learn to support each other's learning and growth. This guide comes with a case scenario and a video demonstration. *Developer: ECTA center, with funding from OSEP*

> http://ectacenter.org/~pdfs/decrp/PG_TC_TeamMembersHelpingOneAnother_prac_print_2017.pdf

Recommended Practices Module 4: Teaming and Collaboration

This module is part of a series of seven interactive modules focused on the DEC Recommended Practices. Each module is designed around the Plan, Do, Study, Act framework. The module introduces the components of teaming and collaboration through short interactive self-paced lessons with video demonstrations of practices and quizzes, activities, and a short scenario-based simulation exercise. There are also learning guides in the instructor area to support faculty and professional development providers to extend the learning. *Developers: Frank Porter Graham Child Development Institute and Puckett Institute with funding from OSEP*

> https://rpm.fpg.unc.edu/module-4-teaming

SpecialQuest Multimedia Training Library: Collaboration and Teaming

This resource is part of a series of modules for professional development providers to support practitioners in implementing high-quality inclusion. This module includes six sessions with activities, videos, and handouts to support practitioners in learning effective team building and collaboration strategies. A presenter's guide and training notes are also included. All the materials within the module are downloadable. *Developer: Hilton/Early Head Start Training Program with funding from the Conrad N. Hilton Foundation and OHS*

> https://eclkc.ohs.acf.hhs.gov/children-disabilities/specialquest/
> collaboration-teaming

The Working Together Series

This series includes five interactive self-paced, self-guided courses for families of children and youths with disabilities and practitioners to learn strategies for working together and through conflict. While the case scenarios in the courses are primarily school-aged examples, the content is also useful and relevant for practitioners working with children ages birth to age 5 and their families. The courses are Introduction to the Working Together Series, Individualized Education Plan (IEP) Meetings and Beyond, Listening and Responding Skills, Managing and Responding to Emotions, and Focusing on Interests to Reach Agreement. Each course also includes facilitator's guides and additional materials for professional development providers to extend the learning. *Developer: The Center for Appropriate Dispute Resolution in Special Education with funding from OSEP*

> https://www.cadreworks.org/resources/cadre-materials/
> working-together-online-learning-series

Using a Primary Service Provider Approach to Teaming

This fact sheet provides information on the evidence-based primary service provider (PSP) approach to teaming in early intervention. Through a Q&A format, this resource addresses confusions about how to identify a PSP, what the roles of the PSP and the rest of the team are, and how to provide sufficient services using a PSP approach to teaming. Though written for physical therapists, all professionals working with young children and their families could apply the PSP approach to teaming with their interdisciplinary early intervention teams. Additional resources and references were also included at the end of the document. *Developer: Section on Pediatrics, American Physical Therapy Association*

> https://pediatricapta.org/includes/fact-sheets/pdfs/13%20Primary%20
> Service%20Provider.pdf

Communication for Collaboration

A Tale of Two Conversations

This resource includes two videos showing a service provider and a family member having a conversation. One shows how a conversation can be difficult when there is a lack of effective communication, and the other shows how the same conversation can be enhanced when both parties use effective communication skills. A study guide is also included to extend the learning. *Developers: Office for Dispute Resolution in Pennsylvania (videos) and The Center for Appropriate*

Dispute Resolution in Special Education (study guide)

> https://www.cadreworks.org/resources/cadre-materials-state-resource/
> tale-two-conversations

CONNECT Module 3: Communication for Collaboration

Part of a series of seven modules focused on evidence-based practices with an emphasis on inclusive settings and meeting the needs of diverse learners, this module focuses on effective communication practices for collaborating with other professionals and families when working with children with disabilities. The module begins with a child care teacher's dilemma about collaborating with a speech therapist to support a young child with disabilities. The module includes video demonstrations of effective communication skills, a research brief, activities, and handouts such as a communication strategies observation checklist. It is also available in Spanish. *Developer: CONNECT: The Center to Mobilize Early Childhood Knowledge, with funding from OSEP*

> http://community.fpg.unc.edu/connect-modules/learners/module-3

Family Practice Guide 2.1: Family Members Working With Other Team Members

Communication with service providers is the first step for families to become active members of their children's intervention teams. Part of a larger set of practice improvement tools to support the use of the DEC Recommended Practices, this learning guide provides detailed practical tips for families as they prepare to communicate with service providers. Included in the guide is a video demonstration and a case scenario of how a family can use communication skills to work effectively with other team members. *Developer: ECTA center, with funding from OSEP*

> http://ectacenter.org/~pdfs/decrp/PG_TC_
> FamilyMembersWorkingwithOtherTeamMembers_family_print_2017.pdf

Practitioner Practice Guide 2.1: Team Members Engaging in Quality Communication

This practice guide provides practitioners with practical tips on how to support quality communications with team members. Part of a larger set of practice improvement tools to support the use of the DEC Recommended Practices, this guide supports practitioners in identifying and using different types of communication formats for clear and effective communication among team members. The guide also includes a video demonstration of the practice. *Developer: ECTA center, with funding from OSEP*

> http://ectacenter.org/~pdfs/decrp/PG_TC_
> TeamMembersEngagingQualityCommunication_prac_print_2017.pdf

Families as Essential Members of the Team

Connect Module 4: Family-Professional Partnerships

This CONNECT module supports practitioners to build trusting family-professional partnerships. The module begins with a child care teacher's dilemma about sharing her concerns about a child with the child's father and a powerful story shared by the child's father, who is a single dad. The module also includes a series of video demonstrations of the stages of building trusting partnerships with families, activities, and handouts, including partnership-oriented practice examples and checklist, family-professional partnership scales, and research and policy briefs on family-professional partnerships. This module is part of a series of seven modules focused on evidence-based practices with an emphasis on inclusive settings and meeting the needs of diverse learners. The modules are also available in Spanish. *Developer: CONNECT: The Center to Mobilize Early Childhood Knowledge, with funding from OSEP*

> http://community.fpg.unc.edu/connect-modules/learners/module-4

Family Guided Routines Based Intervention: Key Indicators

Family-guided routines-based intervention (FGRBI) is an effective early intervention model supported by both research and practice evidence. The FGRBI caregiver-coaching model has four components: setting the stage, observation and opportunities to embed, problem solving and planning, and reflection and review. This resource provides the key indicators for each component, detailed explanations of the indicators, and examples and nonexamples. Early intervention professionals can use this resource as a practice guide for delivering FGRBI and use the checklist in the resource for self-evaluation. *Developers: Juliann Woods, Communication and Early Childhood Research and Practice Center, Florida State University*

> http://fgrbi.fsu.edu/handouts/approach5/KeyIndicatorsManual_2017.pdf

Family Practice Guide 1.1: Participating on Your Child's Team

It is important for families to take an active role and participate fully on their children's team. This learning guide helps family members understand the importance of being a full team member and provides tips and a video demonstration on how to participate and advocate for their children and families. *Developer: ECTA center, with funding from OSEP*

> https://ectacenter.org/~pdfs/decrp/PG_TC_ParticipatingonYourChildsTeam_family_print_2017.pdf

Family Practice Guide 3.1: Sharing What You Know With Professionals

Because family members spend the most time with their children, they have extensive knowledge about their children's development. But how do families effectively share their wealth of knowledge about their child with professionals?

This learning guide provides practical tips, a video demonstration, and a case example of how families can effectively share information with team members and be open to learning new intervention ideas and suggestions proposed by service providers. *Developer: ECTA center, with funding from OSEP*

> http://ectacenter.org/~pdfs/decrp/PG_TC_
> SharingWhatYouKnowwithProfessionals_family_print_2017.pdf

Practitioner Practice Guide 1.1: Helping Families Be Full Team Members

This learning guide provides practitioners with the strategies to engage families and support them in participating fully in assessments, evaluation, IEP/IFSP meetings, and the implementation of plans. The guide also includes a video and a link to an additional resource on partnering with families of children with special needs from the National Association for the Education of Young Children. *Developer: ECTA center, with funding from OSEP*

> http://ectacenter.org/~pdfs/decrp/PG_TC_
> HelpingFamiliesBeFullTeamMembers_prac_print_2017.pdf

Evaluation and Self-Assessment Tools

Brass Tacks: A Self-Rating of Family-Centered Practices in Early Intervention

The Brass Tacks is a self-assessment tool for teams of practitioners who are working with families in early intervention to evaluate their collaboration practices with families. The Brass Tracks contains 78 items covering four areas: initial interactions, assessments, intervention planning, and service provision. This tool provides a comprehensive picture of early intervention team functioning and can support practitioners in assessing how well they are fully including families as team members in the early intervention process and in developing action plans to improve their practices as a team. It is especially useful if families are included in the self-assessment process. *Developers: P.J. McWilliam and Pam Winton, with funding from the Special Education Program of the Office of Special Education and Rehabilitative Services*

> https://fpg.unc.edu/presentations/
> brass-tacks-self-rating-family-centered-practices-early-intervention

Checklists to Support the Use of the DEC Recommended Practices

Part of a larger set of practice improvement tools to support the use of the DEC Recommended Practices, the following three checklists focus on teaming and collaboration.

Collaboration to Learn and Grow Checklist: This checklist provides nine indicators of a team's function in helping members share knowledge and expertise with one another, which can be used not only as an evaluation tool but also as a practice improvement plan. *Developer: ECTA center, with funding from OSEP*

> http://ectacenter.org/~pdfs/decrp/TC-3_Collaboration_Learn_Grow_2018.pdf

Communication for Teaming and Collaboration Checklist: This checklist includes both verbal and written communication skills that are necessary for building relationships and gathering and providing information that can ensure services for children and families are effectively provided. Team members may use it to assess whether effective communication is taking place. *Developer: ECTA center, with funding from OSEP*

> http://ectacenter.org/~pdfs/decrp/TC-2_Communication_Teaming_Collaboration_2018.pdf

Families Are Full Team Members Checklist: This checklist includes 11 descriptors of effective practices to engage families as full team members and can be used by individuals and teams to evaluate the teams' effectiveness in including families during service provision and assess how well families are valued as experts. *Developer: ECTA center, with funding from OSEP*

> http://ectacenter.org/~pdfs/decrp/TC-1_Families_Are_Full_Team_Members_2018.pdf

Skills Inventory for Teams (SIFT)

The Skills Inventory for Teams (SIFT) is intended to support early intervention practitioners in assessing and evaluating their ability to work well with others. The resource provides a list of essential teaming skills at both individual and team levels, covering 12 aspects of team performance. The resource is divided into two parts: (1) team screening and assessment and (2) individual team member screening and assessment. Both parts include a screening scale to identify strengths and needs and an assessment checklist to further determine and define specific needs, which may serve as the foundation for the development of team or individual action plans. *Developers: Corrine Garland, Adrienne Frank, Deana Buck, and Patti Seklemian, with funding from the Handicapped Children's Early Education Program (now known as OSEP)*

> https://files.eric.ed.gov/fulltext/ED361961.pdf

References

Division for Early Childhood. (2014). *DEC recommended practices in early intervention/early childhood special education 2014.* Retrieved from http://www.dec-sped.org/dec-recommended-practices

12

Editorial Team

Editors

Pamela J. Winton, *University of North Carolina at Chapel Hill*
Chelsea Guillen, *University of Illinois at Urbana-Champaign*
Alana G. Schnitz, *Juniper Gardens Children's Project*

Resources Within Reason

Chih-Ing Lim, *Frank Porter Graham Child Development Institute*
Shuting Zheng, *University of California, San Francisco*

Reviewers

Serra Acar, *Western Oregon University*
Rashida Banerjee, *University of Northern Colorado*
Shameka Brown, *University of Illinois at Urbana-Champaign*
Kerry Bull, *Noah's Ark Inc.*
Susan Connor, *University of Illinois at Urbana-Champaign*
John Forster, *Noah's Ark Inc.*
Leslie Fox, *Office of Special Education Programs*
Jessica Hardy, *University of Louisville*
Kathy Heck, *Office of Special Education Programs*
Cori Hill, *Virginia Early Intervention*
Maria Kastanis, *University of Illinois at Urbana-Champaign*
Bernadette Laumann, *University of Illinois at Urbana-Champaign*
Hedi Levine, *Hunter College*
Chih Ing Lim, *Frank Porter Graham Child Development Institute*
Maria Mavrides, *Hunter College*
Rebecca McCathren, *University of Missouri*
Mary McLean, *University of Florida*
Lori Meyer, *University of Vermont*
Megan Purcell, *Purdue University*
Roxane Romanick, *parent, DEC Family Council*
Rosa Milagros Santos, *University of Illinois at Urbana-Champaign*
Kristen Schraml-Block, *University of Illinois at Urbana-Champaign*
Sheila Self, *California Department of Education*
Kimberly Sopko

Judy Swett, *PACER Center*

Kimmie Tang, *California State University, Dominguez Hills*

Anna Wallisch, *University of Kansas*

Jenna Weglarz-Ward, *University of Nevada, Las Vegas*

Kathleen Zimmerman, *University of Kansas*

Index